D1501595

WHEN
IT HURTS
TOO MUCH
TO CRY

When It Hurts

JERRY

with Harold L.

Too Much to Cry

FALWELL

Willmington

Tyndale House
Publishers, Inc.
Wheaton, Illinois

Second printing, February 1985
Library of Congress Catalog Card Number 84-50127
ISBN 0-8423-7993-2
Printed in the United States of America

CONTENTS

PREFACE

When I write or speak, I like to begin with an
explanation of the terms I will use in the discussion.
For example, if I am talking about Bible prophecy, the
Second Coming of Christ, or some other doctrine, I
know that not all my readers or listeners will know
enough theology to understand the words I might use.

But this approach, I think, is not needed for the
subject I now write about. Suffering requires no
explanation whatsoever, for it is as universal to us as
breathing. On any given Lord's Day here at Thomas
Road Baptist Church I could ask the youngest primary
pupils in the Sunday school if they knew what suffering
was, and I would get the right answer. They might say,
"Yes, when the doctor sticks me with a needle, it hurts."
Or, "I cried when I fell and skinned my knee," or "My
tummy ached all last night."

I could ask the oldest members of the church the
same question. "Oh, yes," they would say. "In my sixty
or seventy or ninety years, many sorrows and hours of
suffering have fallen my way."

Retarded teenagers from the local training school
who attend our services could answer the same

question, as could any of our professors at Liberty Baptist College. The answers from each, though couched in different terms, would be identical, for we all know our own kinds of suffering.

We know the *what* of suffering, but we don't always understand the *why*. Regardless of our age, ability, or attitude, we wonder what purpose it accomplishes. Is pain a part of some immutable law of the universe as is the law of gravity? Has it always existed? Will it continue to hound our steps as long as we live? Does it serve any good purpose?

Some partial answers to these very basic questions will be attempted in the pages to follow—partial, I say, because the full reason for pain and suffering remains a dark, undeclared secret, locked in the bosom of God, to be revealed only on the other side of eternity.

This book deals with the suffering experienced by the child of God. Such horrors as the Nazi holocaust, the starvation of millions of innocent children in the world, the horrors of war, or other tragedies demand their own explanations. Right now, let us limit ourselves to a discussion of pain and sorrow in the lives of believers.

CHAPTER ONE

The Mystery of Suffering

CLIFFORD felt God calling him to enter the ministry. He left his well-paying job in North Carolina and moved to Lynchburg with his wife and two small sons. As soon as they got settled in, he began his studies in the two-year Bible program at Liberty. His wife, in addition to her excellent spiritual qualities, was a very good secretary, and soon began working for one of the vice-presidents at Liberty Baptist College.

Both were doing well. Clifford proved to be an excellent student and finished his first semester with honors. As their pastor, I was proud of this dedicated and loving family and the contribution everyone thought they were going to make in serving the Lord.

But one Saturday night in April, just a few minutes after Clifford had finished family devotions with his wife and children, something happened that made absolutely no sense to any of us. Someone standing outside fired a shotgun point-blank at Clifford through the living room window, killing him instantly.

I arrived on the scene a few minutes after it happened. The small living room of this lovely couple, who showed no desire in the world but to serve and obey Jesus, had suddenly been turned into a horror chamber. How could God have allowed such a terrible thing to happen?

I have thought about Clifford and his lovely family many times. I'm certain all of us at some time have turned to the Scriptures for answers to similar questions.

After we have examined the Bible and every other logical piece of information at our disposal we seem to come to the same conclusion. The reason for some of the suffering we see will remain an unsolvable mystery, unknown and unknowable in this life. With this in mind, I think Christian leaders often do their people a disservice when they spout glib and shallow clichés to people going through some of these dark experiences.

We might wish that Clifford had been the only person we ever knew whose death leaves us with unanswered questions, but that is not the case. Another young man named Steve came to Lynchburg to prepare for the mission field. He had already spent some time in a foreign country with one of the evangelistic groups sponsored by the college. Steve was a faithful student and active in personal evangelism.

During his junior year, Steve left Lynchburg to spend the Christmas holidays with his parents, who lived in one of the western states.

But Steve never arrived home. A few days later his abandoned car was found alongside a highway in Ohio. Following a long search, they discovered his remains in a wooded area near where his car had been found.

No one ever found out exactly what happened. Apparently he had picked up a hitchhiker, perhaps to witness to him. If so, it seems the very person he was trying to help took advantage of him. A young man who wanted more than anything else to give his life to God's service ended up as what appeared to be a total waste on a lonely roadside in the hands of a ruthless killer.

Again we may ask the question: "What possible divine purpose was involved in this?"

There is an old spiritual song which begins with the words: "Nobody knows the trouble I've seen. Nobody knows but Jesus." The truth is, others have gone through the same kinds of trials we have faced and are facing. The Apostle Paul wrote: "There hath no temptation taken you but such as is common to man . . ." (1 Cor. 10:13). There is nothing new under the sun. In all probability, the very troubles, sorrows, and pain that overwhelm any of us at this moment are the same troubles that others have known. The children of God do suffer from time to time. But it doesn't mean that God has forgotten us. We need to remember that God's love and mercy and his ministering angels are usually much closer to us when we are in pain and in deep spiritual need than at those times when we are feeling spiritually strong.

The Bible is filled with stories of suffering. The Old Testament tells of Job's physical agony, of Hezekiah's near fatal attack of boils, of those who suffered with leprosy and other illnesses. Jesus ministered to many who were suffering with dropsy, fevers, blindness, lameness, and palsy.

Women through all ages, such as Sarah, Hannah, and Elizabeth, have felt the hurtful stigma of barrenness. Others, such as Dinah and Tamar, have undergone the terrible ordeal and suffering of rape.

Many have suffered unfair persecutions, imprisonments, beatings, stonings, hangings, being put into lions' dens. Others have been tortured, beheaded, enslaved, burned at the stake.

The Bible tells the life stories of people who seemed to have been called to special ministries of suffering— men like Joseph, Jeremiah, Job, and the Apostle Paul,

all of whom we will study more closely in later
chapters.

We can see clearly that the Bible talks much about the
problem of pain, suffering, and death. It should be
reassuring for us to know that God has had so much
experience in dealing with his people who have
suffered in the past.

The first question many people ask about suffering
has to do with its origin. Where does it come from? For
that answer we have to go to the Scriptures.

THE ORIGIN

For the past several years I have been invited to some
of America's oldest and most influential secular
universities to address the students on such topics as
morality, fundamentalism, and other issues. Often some
cynical remarks about the Bible and other insults are
shouted at me by a noisy few, even as I am trying to
speak. One remark often heard is, "I don't believe the
Bible, because there are lies in it."

To deal with such comments about the Bible, I agree
with the students. "You are right," I told one young
man. "There are indeed lies in the Bible, and your
problem is that you are a victim of the very first one."

To say the least, I got his attention. I went on to
explain that, while the Word of God does not in any
way teach or sanction lies, it nevertheless does, on
several occasions, accurately record various lies as
uttered by false witnesses.

For example, the very first lie in the Bible, found in
Genesis 3:4, has to do with suffering and death. God
had previously warned Adam and Eve that to disobey
and eat of the forbidden fruit would result in death
(Gen. 2:17). But Satan brazenly told Eve, "Ye shall not

surely die." That, of course, was a lie, perhaps the greatest lie of all time.

But what does this have to do with suffering? In a nutshell, it has everything to do with it, because when Adam and Eve believed that lie and disobeyed God, sin came into the world. Having found the necessary fertile soil, sin immediately produced the bitter fruit of suffering. Every tear and tragedy, from cancer to the common cold, from broken bones to broken hearts, can be directly traced back to that terrible moment in the Garden of Eden. It is simply impossible to overstate the devastating results and the untold sorrow sin has produced.

The first symptoms of sin for Adam and Eve were fear and alienation. Realizing his nakedness, panic-stricken Adam attempted to hide himself from God among the trees of Eden. What loneliness and isolation he must have suffered as he hid behind his fig leaves, not knowing what terrible things the future would hold! But that was just the beginning. In a short time, Adam and Eve would experience a double agony, that of burying their youngest son, who had been murdered by his older brother. Only eternity will reveal the sadness these first parents felt at this the world's first funeral service.

This suffering and death was just the first installment payment on the staggering debt demanded by the judgment against their sin. We might dramatize what, in effect, happened to them.

ADAM: *Who's out there? What do you want?*
INTRUDER: *You've never met me, I know. But I'd like to come in and help straighten you two out about some of your outdated hang-ups about obedience. Go ahead and eat those goodies if you want, "for God doth know that*

in the day ye eat thereof, then your eyes shall be opened, and ye shall be as gods, knowing good and evil."

ADAM: *Well, I guess it's all right. But remember, this is more my wife's idea than mine.*

(Adam allows the intruder and his ideas in. But as soon as Adam and his wife eat the fruit, there appear two vicious and horrible-looking individuals.)

ADAM: *Who are you two? Where did you come from?*

FIRST MONSTER: *I am Physical Death and sin sent me. I've come to plague your bodies with ailments, injuries, pain, anger, loneliness, despair, frustration, and whatever other tortures I can think of. In the end, I'll yank your souls from your bodies and dump your corpses into a grave.*

SECOND MONSTER: *I'm Spiritual Death and sin also sent me. I'm ten times meaner than Physical Death. I intend to fill you with the dread of dying and to keep you from knowing and believing God. My ultimate goal is to land you right in the middle of the eternal lake of fire.*

Of course, this conversation never actually took place, but theologically it expresses exactly what happened when Adam and Eve sinned. We may not have asked for any of the suffering and pain we are going through at this moment, and it may not, in any way, be a result of sin we have committed. But ultimately, we must trace all suffering, sickness, and pain back to where it started, with that first lie of Satan and the first sin of Adam and Eve.

When Christians suffer, other questions often arise, such as "How can a good God allow it to happen?" I hear this often, especially when those closest to the pain seem to have done nothing to deserve it, and when the cause of suffering appears to be a hindrance to God's work.

A young man named Danny finished up at the seminary here in Lynchburg and left for Alabama with his young family to begin an exciting new ministry. A new church had called him as pastor, and he had just finished his first official duty there by conducting their New Year's Eve Watch Night Service. It had been a wonderful time of fellowship and testimony, with both pastor and people eagerly looking forward to the spiritual challenges of the new year.

Among those who attended the Watch Night Service was a Liberty Baptist Seminary professor and his wife. He had been one of Danny's teachers at the seminary, and they were staying overnight with Danny and his family. After their wives had gone to bed, the two men spent the remaining hours of that first early morning discussing the potential of this wonderful new church.

Suddenly, a disturbing noise was heard coming from the bedroom. Rushing in, the men found Danny's wife gasping for breath. In spite of their frantic efforts, she died a few minutes later.

Scarcely twelve hours had gone by in his role as pastor of this congregation before Danny was left a widower with a small child. Can we really believe a good God would allow such a tragedy to occur?

As the former pastor of this young couple, I have no idea whatsoever just why such apparent disasters are permitted, and neither does anyone else!

But I do know this—someday in the glories of eternal heaven, God will tenderly gather this young couple and their child along with their loved ones and, in loving and logical terms, fully explain to each of them all of his purposes in what was, humanly speaking, a tragedy.

The poem called *The Weaver,* though old and often quoted, remains a favorite because it contains so much truth about the way God works in the painful affairs of this life:

THE WEAVER

My life is but a weaving
  Between my Lord and me;
I cannot choose the colors
  He worketh steadily.

Ofttimes He weaveth sorrow
  And I in foolish pride,
Forget that He seeth the upper,
  And I the under side.

Not till the loom is silent
  And the shuttles cease to fly,
Shall God unroll the canvas
  And explain the reason why.

The dark threads are as needful
  In the Weaver's skillful hand,
As the threads of gold and silver
  In the pattern He has planned.

—Author unknown

We must conclude that suffering and pain are allowed by God. The next question is, "To what degree am I responsible for the suffering I'm now undergoing?"

To answer this question we need to examine the various immediate causes of pain and suffering.

IMMEDIATE SOURCES

We suffer because we have a fallen nature. We have previously traced all suffering back to the Garden of

Eden and Adam's sin. When the first couple disobeyed God, something drastic happened to their physical bodies. Their flesh became open season to every harmful bacteria and every disease-producing virus on earth. In fact, the very cells of their bodies began to suffer a traumatic reprogramming which would by itself cause aging, infirmities, and ultimate death.

Until the glorious resurrection, this deadly process of physical deterioration even in believers cannot be reversed but can only be delayed through medicine and surgery. In reality, therefore, each birthday celebration should also serve as a reminder to us of our approaching death day.

One of the glorious results of the second birth means that the Holy Spirit has come to make us spiritually new creatures. As Paul phrased it, "Therefore if any man be in Christ, he is a new creature: old things are passed away; behold, all things are become new" (2 Cor. 5:17).

However, lest we forget, until the coming resurrection the child of God also retains the same physical body with all its sinful desires. Paul struggled, as we all do, against these physical desires, which he called "the flesh." In some detail he recorded the struggle for us: "For that which I do I allow not: for what I would, that do I not; but what I hate, that do I. . . . For to will is present with me; but how to perform that which is good I find not. . . . For I delight in the law of God after the inward man: But I see another law in my members, warring against the law of my mind, and bringing me into captivity to the law of sin which is in my members" (Rom. 7:15, 18, 22, 23).

Paul described to the Galatians the same conflict between the new spirit within him and the flesh which remained in him: "For the flesh lusteth against the

Spirit, and the Spirit against the flesh: and these are contrary the one to the other: so that ye cannot do the things that ye would" (Gal. 5:17).

Along with our fallen flesh, we suffer also from our fallen minds. Man's thought processes were drastically affected by the Fall. He could now be tormented by intense mental suffering, perhaps even more excruciating than the physical, such as fear, guilt, despair, grief, remorse, and depression. As any medical doctor would testify, literally millions of otherwise healthy bodies have physically deteriorated before their time because of the tormented minds that controlled them.

Ungodly people cause us to suffer. This book is not large enough to contain even the names of all the believers who have died because of their testimony for Christ. Because the ungodly hate Christ, they unleash persecutions, ridicule, job discrimination, social ostracism, even violence on those who belong to Christ. Jesus warned his followers, "And ye shall be betrayed . . . and some of you shall they cause to be put to death. And ye shall be hated of all men for my name's sake" (Luke 21:16, 17).

The writer of Hebrews, describing those who had been persecuted, said, "And others had trial of cruel mockings and scourgings, yea, moreover of bonds and imprisonment: they were stoned, they were sawn asunder . . . being destitute, afflicted, tormented (of whom the world was not worthy:) they wandered in deserts, and in mountains, and in dens and caves of the earth . . ." (Heb. 11:36-38).

Paul himself suffered at the hands of ungodly men: "Alexander the coppersmith did me much evil: the Lord reward him according to his works" (2 Tim. 4:14). The very nature of ungodly men is to despise godliness and those who desire to live godly lives, so we should not be surprised when their evil intentions spill over onto us.

Suffering is caused by the world system. Can you imagine an eagle suddenly bound and forced to live its life in the water like a duck? How uncomfortable and unnatural such a life would be! This creature of the air was designed by its divine Creator to soar in the heavens, to feel the warmth of the sun, and to make its bed among the lofty mountain heights. Imagine how miserable it would be, cold and wet, struggling in a hostile watery nest, totally alien to its nature.

In some ways, man can be compared to the eagle. Man alone was created in the image of God. To man alone was given the command to subdue all things, which included the birds of the air and the fish of the sea. But since the Fall, the subduer has become the subdued. Through the sin of disobedience, man's beautiful home in Eden degenerated to an environment almost as alien to him as water to the eagle. The child of God dwells at this present time in an unnatural and hostile world system.

In the Old Testament we read of Lot, living in a perverted city, Sodom, aware of terrible pressures from a wicked world system. In his second epistle, Peter wrote of him: "For that righteous man dwelling among them, in seeing and hearing, vexed his righteous soul from day to day with their unlawful deeds" (2 Pet. 2:8).

Paul warned believers not to be "conformed to this world" (Rom. 12:2), referring to the world system (Greek: *cosmos*). John exhorted, "Love not the world [*cosmos*], neither the things that are in the world"

(1 John 2:15). A world system that was hostile to Jesus will also be hostile to the children of God.

Suffering is caused by satanic activity. In describing the work of Christ to the Roman convert Cornelius, Peter said, "God anointed Jesus of Nazareth with the Holy Ghost and with power: who went about doing good, and healing all that were oppressed of the devil; for God was with him" (Acts 10:38). Notice the phrase, "all that were oppressed of the devil." There is no doubt that some of the suffering we encounter is a direct result of satanic activity. Both Satan and his fallen angels can heap intense discomfort upon believers. Paul said that Satan prevented him on one occasion from visiting the church in Thessalonica (1 Thess. 2:18), and inflicted him with a thorn in the flesh (2 Cor. 12:7). We have also read of the agony inflicted on Job by the devil.

During Christ's ministry, he once healed a woman on the Sabbath day. When the synagogue leader criticized him, the Lord responded, "Ought not this woman, being a daughter of Abraham, whom Satan hath bound, lo, these eighteen years, be loosed from this bond on the sabbath day?" (Luke 13:16).

While it would be inaccurate to say that all affliction is directly produced by Satan and his fallen angels, the Bible on several occasions clearly attributed insanity (Mark 5:15), muteness of speech (Matt. 9:33), deafness (Mark 9:25), epilepsy (Matt. 17:15-18), and blindness (Matt. 12:22) to satanic activity. Probably only a very small fraction of these ailments today are produced by Satan but we can see that it is possible.

Other Christians cause us to suffer. Few will disagree that the most crushing mental pain felt by a Christian can come from another Christian. To be unfairly criticized and mistreated by those belonging to the same family of God and household of faith can be almost unbearable.

One of the ways in which Jesus had to suffer was in seeing his disciples flee when trouble came and in hearing Peter deny him in the courtyard of the high priest's house when Jesus was on trial.

After my graduation from a well-known Christian school, I came back to my hometown, Lynchburg, Virginia, for a short visit, planning to start a church in another state. However, a small group of believers in this city felt God wanted me to become their pastor. After much prayer and fasting, I received from the Lord the same assurance, so I accepted their call. I didn't know it then, but that was the beginning of much heartache for me. The problem stemmed from the fact that there was already in the city another church with the same denominational background as mine. The pastor complained of the impending competition, and upon hearing of it, the officials from the school where I graduated issued an ultimatum, forbidding me to assume leadership of the new church. Going a step further, they threatened to exclude me from their fellowship if I ignored their warning.

The pressure soon became almost unbearable, for these were my former spiritual leaders, godly men who had taught me everything I knew about the ministry. How could I deny their criticism? If I did go ahead, I wondered if I could possibly survive without their prayers and support. But the more I prayed and fasted, the greater assurance I had that God had indeed called me to Lynchburg. So with some anxiety, but compensated by God's assurance, I stepped out on faith and assumed the pastorate of the Thomas Road Baptist Church.

All of this happened some twenty-seven years ago. Today the church has nearly 20,000 members, a college with enrollment exceeding 4,000, an annual budget of some $80 million, and a worldwide radio and television ministry. I believe God vindicated my decision back then. And I can add that the old wounds with my brothers in Christ have long since been healed and that sweet Christian fellowship has been restored. But at the time I learned the terrible discomfort one can feel as a victim of well-intended but unfounded criticism from fellow believers.

There is a story of a boxer who was having a very difficult time during a boxing match. He was being pummeled quite badly by his opponent round after round. In between rounds his manager was trying to encourage him. "Don't worry. I can tell you, he's getting winded. He's not laying a hand on you!"

The bewildered fighter replied, "Then for goodness sake, keep an eye on that referee, for somebody out there is hitting me pretty hard!"

Like the boxer, it seems on occasion, we keep getting pounded without letup, and sometimes we can't tell exactly where the pain is coming from. But we can be certain, as Job later learned, it has all come with God's permission. Jesus knows that we also suffer, "For in that he himself hath suffered being tempted, he is able to succour them that are tempted" (Heb. 2:18).

CHAPTER TWO

How the World Answers to Suffering

BECAUSE suffering is both universal and unsettling, it is not surprising that we find many attempted answers to the dilemma of pain. Some answers are part of widespread philosophies bordering on religions, while others are man's attempts to explain or rationalize his own experience.

REINCARNATION

Eastern religions, which believe that all life forms are reincarnated beings from an earlier existence, conclude that someone who undergoes great suffering in this life is probably being punished for the sins of his or her former existence. In the same way, those who are born to relative ease and prosperity are, in some way, being rewarded for their goodness in a former life state.

If this were true, think what terrible people Joseph, Job, Jeremiah, Paul, and Jesus were in their former lives to merit what they endured in their earthly lives!

COSMIC DUALISM

Like the philosophy of reincarnation, dualism is a vital plank in the platform of many Eastern religions. In essence, it holds that there are two gods (or principles) governing the universe, one good and the other bad. The evil god is in control during the present age, providing an explanation for the presence of pain, suffering, and evil in the world today. According to this system, those who resist the evil of this age will enter a future age of righteousness and be recompensed by the good god.

The Gnostics of Paul's day and of the following centuries held to a form of dualism, which taught that the spirit was basically good and that the physical world, including the physical body, was evil. This would explain to them the presence of evil and suffering here in the physical realm.

FATALISM

The Islamic community, with its hundreds of millions, accepts the most frightful suffering with a shrug of the shoulders and a comment, "It is the will of Allah!"

Fatalism is a form of belief in fate, a blind power of destiny which controls the universe, including human liberty. The doctrine of absolute predestination, the strong view that God controls in both the means and ends of everything, somewhat resembles the pagan view of fate. The Bible writers, however, in discussing God's sovereignty never omitted from their teaching man's responsibility for his choices or guilt for his sins.

The philosophy of existentialism, with its nihilistic perspective, much like fatalism, views pain and suffering as part of the senseless and useless existence man has on earth. Whether one believes as a fatalist, that some blind power is controlling the means and ends to everything, or whether one is a nihilist, pain and suffering are thought of as matters completely beyond our comprehension and control, and thus they have no purpose or meaning that concerns us.

HEDONISM
Hedonism is the philosophy which holds that pleasure or happiness is the sole good in life. The modern playboy philosophy is a form of hedonism. To someone who is suffering, the hedonist would suggest that pleasure be substituted for pain—sex, money, power, drugs, or whatever else might be found to displace painful thoughts or feelings.

NATURALISM
The theory denying that any effect or object has a supernatural significance is called naturalism or evolutionism. This view holds that suffering, like digestion, is a part of life. We are assured that for some unknown reason, those accidental and uncaring mechanical forces which brought life out of nothing and into existence, also programmed life organisms to suffer before they eventually pass into oblivion. According to naturalism, suffering and death are no more significant than a mature tree falling in the untracked wilderness.

STOICISM
Stoicism holds that wise people should be free from passion, unmoved by joy or grief, and submissive to natural law. Such a philosophy could also be part of the view of Fatalism or Dualism, since it refers to man's response to the world around him.

This philosophy began around 300 B.C., but many forms of it exist today, even among some believers. People who have been deeply hurt, instead of properly dealing with their inner feelings, make all kinds of attempts to stop feeling anything, good or bad.

An attitude of stoicism is often an attempt to show personal strength in the face of adversity, the kind reflected in the often-quoted poem by W. E. Henley:

INVICTUS

Out of the night that covers me,
  Black as the pit from pole to pole,
I thank whatever gods there be
  For my unconquerable soul.

In the fell clutch of circumstance,
  I have not winced nor cried aloud,
Under the bludgeonings of chance
  My head is bloody, but unbowed.

Beyond this place of wrath and tears
  Looms but the horror of the shade;
And yet the menace of the years
  Finds, and shall find, me unafraid.

It matters not how strait the gate,
  How charged with punishments the scroll
I am the master of my fate;
  I am the captain of my soul!

CHRISTIAN SCIENCE

According to Mary Baker Eddy, the founder of this religious cult, the solution to pain and suffering is to utterly deny its presence, for in reality, neither pain,

suffering, or the physical body exist, except as an error
of mortal mind, an error in thinking.

This belief is very much like a form of psychological
adjustment which is called *denial*. Some people who
have heard bad news, or who have the symptoms of a
dread disease, will actually deny the existence of pain
or painful realities. This form of hysteria can continue
for long periods of time, if not permanently.

BAD THEOLOGY

Any incorrect view of God can keep persons from
properly dealing with suffering. If, for example, one
believed that God did not have the power to control the
universe, he would believe that God had pity for him in
his suffering but was otherwise helpless to do anything
about it. If someone did not think that God, along with
being a God of justice, was a God of love and mercy,
he would expect God to inflict us only with suffering.
To such a person, sorrow and suffering could be directly
traced back to an indifferent, uncaring, unfeeling,
unloving deity.

Another incorrect doctrine is the view that all sorrow
and pain is punishment for personal sin. This view rests
on two basic assumptions.

First, we are sometimes incorrectly taught that it is
never in the will of God for a Christian to suffer or to
be sick, especially if the suffering is physical. The
second assumption, the false conclusion drawn from the
first, is that if there is suffering in the believer's life, it
must be directly attributed to some personal sin. Of all
the hurtful philosophies or doctrines about suffering,
this one may be the most cruel and hateful of them all!

One of the most well-known faith healers of this

century once said that he based his entire healing ministry on the verse: "Beloved, I wish above all things that thou mayest prosper and be in health, even as thy soul prospereth" (3 John 2).

This preacher said that as a young man he carefully studied this verse and had concluded that God wanted the bodies of Christians to be as saved from pain and suffering as their souls were saved from Satan and hell. While I do seriously question his interpretation of this passage of Scripture, I don't for one moment question his sincerity.

Such a view, that God delivers us from all sickness and pain, is based on how one understands the meaning and purpose of the atonement of Christ. Nearly every evangelical theologian would accept the idea that all good—every benefit we have—is based on the goodness of God made possible and available to us through the atonement, Christ's death on the cross. But the implication that sickness is a result of personal sin goes much further, claiming that Christ's death on the cross was intended to bring health to our physical bodies just as it was to bring spiritual health to our souls. By this logic, one could say that God, who has committed himself to save all those who call on him, is also committed to heal everyone who calls on him.

The controversy is an old one, but most theologians today agree that such a view is based on misinterpretation of the Bible, as I believe the case to be in the verse quoted earlier.

In its proper context, as one can see from the most casual reading, John was simply saying to his friend Gaius the words we often use to begin our letters today:

Dear _____ ,
I hope this letter finds you in good health.

This view, that all suffering is caused by personal sin, is not a new one. In fact, we see a detailed account of it more than four thousand years ago, as described in the Book of Job.

Upon hearing of the terrible trials of their friend, Eliphaz, Bildad, and Zophar came to visit the patriarch to help him through his time of extreme suffering. Each one brought his own counsel, based on a slightly different premise. Eliphaz (4:12-17) approached the problem on the basis of personal experience. Bildad (8:8) argued on the basis of tradition, and Zophar (11:6) took a strong dogmatic position, based on his view of God and his righteousness. But all three arrived at the same conclusion, namely that God does not permit the righteous to suffer, and since Job was suffering, then Job was guilty of some secret sin (22:23; 8:5, 6; 11:13-15).

In spite of his pitiful cries and denials, the three friends remained sympathetic but firm in their cruel accusations. Their only advice was that Job should confess whatever he was doing wrong and end his needless suffering.

Job's wife, accepting the same view, felt that Job should curse God, and let God strike him dead, which would end his suffering. Evidently she felt certain wrongdoing had brought him to the brink of death, so he should commit one final sin which would push him across the brink into the relief of oblivion.

In the end, God had to step in and set the record straight, severely rebuking the three men for their false and unfounded counsel. "The Lord said to Eliphaz the Temanite, My wrath is kindled against thee, and against thy two friends: for ye have not spoken of me the thing that is right, as my servant Job hath" (Job 42:7). This verse shows that God has other reasons for suffering than punishment for personal sins.

Centuries later, in the New Testament, a similar situation arose, but on this occasion it was Jesus' disciples who expressed the same basic attitude as Job's friends. One day the disciples and Jesus came upon a blind beggar. As they watched the wretched man, squatting beside the way in sightless desperation, they asked Jesus: "Master, who did sin, this man, or his parents, that he was born blind?" (John 9:2).

Why such a question? It was obvious that they had arrived at the same mistaken conclusion as Job's friends. The man was blind, they reasoned, and suffering had to be the result of sin—either this man's or his parents'.

Jesus quickly corrected this totally false philosophy. While it is true that some of our sins, and some of our parents' sins can cause suffering for us, it is not always true. "Jesus answered, Neither hath this man sinned, nor his parents: but that the works of God should be made manifest in him" (John 9:3).

There are many possible reasons for suffering. Sometimes others bring it on us. Sometimes suffering really is the consequence of personal sin. But we can see that Jesus taught that suffering is sometimes only for the purpose of glorifying God.

Later in Jesus' ministry we read of the death of Lazarus. Again Christ stressed this all-important truth. When Lazarus first became ill, his sisters sent for Jesus to come and heal him. "When Jesus heard that, he said, This sickness is not unto death, but for the glory of

God, that the Son of God might be glorified thereby"
(John 11:4).

As all of the above views testify, suffering is not
always directly related to sin. But man continues to try
to find an answer for suffering, even if no answer
readily presents itself.

Sometimes the answers to our questions about
suffering are slow in coming, but a God who is loving
and merciful will, we can be sure, tell us in his own
time and when it is for our good to know.

CHAPTER THREE

Joseph
the Sufferer

YOUNG people at various secular universities I have visited often ask, "If your God is all-knowing, why did he allow suffering to enter the world?" Or, "If God is all-caring, as you say, why doesn't he put an end to suffering?"

An earlier chapter offered a partial answer to the first question. The Bible shows us some of the reasons, but for other instances of suffering, we will have to wait until God specifically answers for us.

One of the best ways to understand suffering is to look at people in the Bible who have suffered and try to see what God was doing in their lives. Since God never changes, the way he deals with people will not change.

One such biblical example is Joseph, the eleventh son of the patriarch Jacob. Since Joseph was the first child of Rachel, Jacob's favorite wife, Joseph became a favored son: "Now Israel [Jacob] loved Joseph more than all his children, because he was the son of his old age: and he made him a coat of many colours [garment with sleeves]" (Gen. 37:3).

Some argument could be made that Joseph was also, in one sense, God's favorite of Jacob's sons. Since Joseph was the firstborn son of the wife Jacob had chosen for himself, Jacob's special love for Joseph can be understood. Leah had been forced on Jacob by his father-in-law. The barrenness of Rachel caused Jacob to take the handmaidens of Rachel and Leah. But it seems as if Rachel was the only wife Jacob would have taken had his father-in-law Laban not tricked him.

When the land of Israel was divided up centuries later, it appeared that God allotted to Joseph's descendants what might be considered a double portion normally due a firstborn son. Both Ephraim and Manasseh received equal status among the tribes with the other sons of Jacob.

Early in Joseph's life, God gave him two dreams, both of which suggested that the day would come when all the sons of Jacob would bow down to Joseph. While the way Joseph chose to reveal the meaning of the dreams to his brothers may not have been very tactful, the dreams were an accurate revelation of what was to come, as the story in Genesis later revealed.

Because of the special favor received from his father and the anger of his brothers over the dreams, they mistreated him, selling him to some Midianites who were passing by (37:28). To cover their sin, they told their father Jacob that Joseph had been killed (37:31-35). Later Joseph was sold by the Midianite traders to a high Egyptian official, Potiphar.

In Egypt, Joseph served his master well and became a trusted steward in the household. Potiphar's wife on several occasions tried to seduce the young man, but because of Joseph's integrity, he stood clear of any sinful involvement with her. Finally, in anger Potiphar's wife accused Joseph of raping her, and innocent Joseph was put in prison, where he stayed for more than two years.

In prison, Joseph befriended some of his cellmates,

both of whom had dreams which Joseph correctly interpreted. As Joseph had predicted, one of the men was executed but the other was freed, but promptly forgot Joseph in jail.

The Scriptures tell us, "But the Lord was with Joseph, and shewed him mercy, and gave him favour in the sight of the keeper of the prison. . . . The keeper of the prison looked not to any thing that was under his hand; because the Lord was with him [Joseph], and that which he did, the Lord made it to prosper" (Gen. 39:21, 23).

Betrayed by his own brothers, sold into slavery, betrayed by his master's wife, and forgotten in jail— plenty of cause to be bitter. But in spite of his suffering, Joseph's testimony shines out as an example of what we can learn to do when we are wrongly treated by others.

SUFFERING GLORIFIES GOD
Christians can learn much from Joseph's suffering. Perhaps one of the best lessons to understand is that some suffering in our lives is for no other obvious purpose but to glorify God. In spite of all he endured, Joseph remained an example of what God can do in us to glorify himself if we allow him.

This truth about that kind of suffering was one of the hard lessons that Cindy learned. It was Christmas, and Cindy, one of our secretaries here at Liberty Baptist College, was very excited, not with just the celebration of the birth of Christ. She and her husband, after five years of marriage, were going to have their first child.

They were having their usual big Christmas celebration at her mother's home. About mid-afternoon Cindy became more and more uncomfortable, and by six o'clock, it was obvious that she would have to go to the hospital.

At the hospital, the nurses put her immediately on the table and moments later she delivered a one pound, ten ounce baby boy. The doctor said, "He's an awfully small child, and we'll do what we can, but don't get your hopes up." A couple of hours later, she and her husband were allowed to see him. He was tiny, and appeared bruised, but to them he was beautiful, because he was theirs, and a symbol of their love and union.

That was the only time they saw the child. At five o'clock the next morning they were told the child had died. It was very painful, as one might imagine. But, they both believed God had a purpose—and it might be a purpose they would not fully understand right away.

For weeks, even months after the baby died, little things—a diaper commercial or a song on the radio—would bring tears to Cindy's eyes.

In time Cindy and her husband recognized that some very good things had happened as a result of their baby's death. They realized how weak their relationship to Jesus Christ had been.

Sometimes it takes a tragedy to make people realize that God might have to allow something to happen "to us" to help us understand what he wants to do "in us" or "through us." Only time will tell how many heartbroken couples Cindy and her husband may touch with their own experience-tested faith in Christ.

When Joseph was suffering, like Cindy and her husband, there was no way to know the purposes behind the suffering until later. More important than the pain itself in God's eyes is how we respond to it.

"We still don't understand why God allowed it to happen," Cindy said recently, "but we hope that through this experience those who don't know the Lord might see that he has been our source of strength during this difficult time."

Joseph refused to compromise. No matter how others treated him, Joseph remained the same. Others might have said, "Well, what difference does it make? I might as well go ahead and have fun out of life. I tried to live right all my life and look what it's gotten me." But Joseph remained true, despite the temptation to be bitter and to give in to the persuasions of Potiphar's wife.

Joseph bore his suffering patiently. Two years is a long time. One might wonder what he was thinking through all those days in prison. Was he wondering about his family? Was he worried how his aged father was bearing up under the bad news of his supposed death? All that we really know about that period of time is that Joseph kept busy and did the best he could. He was a faithful, hard-working servant in Potiphar's house and he was a trusted servant even in prison.

Sometimes patience and endurance are required for long-term physical conditions, as Reva Arnold, another secretary at Liberty Baptist College, has learned.

From the time she was born, Reva has suffered from chronic allergies. For years, at Christmas, rather than celebrating with her family, she spent many hours in the hospital with chronic bronchitis and pneumonia, not realizing she was severely allergic to evergreen Christmas trees.

At fourteen years of age, Reva was back in the

hospital for major abdominal surgery. In later years a car accident left her with severe spinal injuries.

It is hard to imagine what long hospitalizations and continual health problems can do to the human spirit. For months Reva lay in bed, cried a lot, and wondered if she would ever be able to do anything worthwhile with her life. Many times she prayed, "Lord, why? I don't understand." She knew God didn't make mistakes, but the answer for her problems didn't come.

The questions returned as further complications with her abdominal problems required more surgery, leaving her with the knowledge that she could never have children of her own.

Someone like Reva must learn, as she did, to say, "I have not endured what some other people have had to endure, but if there is someone out there who has had a similar problem, I hope they can learn from God's work in my life that he is sufficient for all our needs."

Joseph maintained a good testimony. Rather than complain and avoid the harshness of his slavery and imprisonment, Joseph seemed to make the best of it, not just doing what he had to do, but doing his tasks in such an exemplary fashion that he was given greater responsibilities. Potiphar put him in charge of the entire household (39:2-4), and the jailor put him in charge of all the other inmates (39:21, 22).

Joseph ministered to other sufferers. Rather than being concerned for himself and his unfair treatment, Joseph was sensitive to the needs of others. Suffering people often concern themselves with their own problems, but when Joseph saw that the other prisoners were sad, he wanted to know why and what he could do about it (40:6-8).

Joseph was a good forgiver. The day finally came when
Joseph's questions about his suffering were answered.
When famine struck the land of Canaan, Jacob sent his
sons into Egypt to buy grain. After they came before
Joseph, he eventually arranged for the entire family to
be moved into the grassy lands of Egypt where they
could stay with their cattle, sheep, and goats. Joseph
had every reason to be angry, and every opportunity to
take vengeance on his brothers. But he didn't.

It could have been at the reunion with his family that
the truth dawned on him as to why God had allowed it
all to happen. From his difficulty had come the
salvation of his family.

Joseph reassured his frightened brothers, "Now
therefore be not grieved, nor angry with yourselves,
that ye sold me hither: for God did send me before you
to preserve life. . . . And God sent me before you to
preserve you a posterity in the earth, and to save your
lives by a great deliverance. So now it was not you that
sent me hither, but God" (45:5, 7, 8).

Later when Jacob died, his brothers became fearful
again, thinking that Joseph would then remember their
evil and take vengeance. But again Joseph reassured
them, saying, "Fear not. . . . But as for you, ye thought
evil against me; but God meant it unto good, to bring
to pass, as it is this day, to save much people alive.
Now therefore fear ye not: I will nourish you, and your
little ones. And he comforted them, and spake kindly
unto them" (50:19-21).

SUFFERING PREPARES FOR GREATER MINISTRY

In many ways Joseph's life is similar to another giant of
God who came along years later. Elijah would one day
stand on Mt. Carmel and challenge all the prophets of

Baal in a contest and God would vindicate him by consuming the offering on the stone altar. Before that day of exaltation there had to come a period of humiliation as part of his training.

Humiliation generally comes before exaltation. For days Elijah had to be fed by ravens, scavenger birds. Then for some time after that he had to be cared for by a penniless widow (1 Kings 17). What a frustrating time this must have been for Elijah, this man of action. But it was necessary as part of his divine preparation. Finally the big day arrived, and Elijah had successfully completed the course of humiliation. Then and only then could he be greatly used of God.

Later in the story of Elijah we read that he restored the widow's son to life (1 Kings 17:22). This was the first time in all history a resurrection had taken place. Who would have thought that God would use a man whose own life had to be sustained by ravens and a helpless widow?

Later Elijah demonstrated the person and power of the only true God to both the people of God and the pagan Baal worshipers on Mt. Carmel. This was quite an accomplishment for a man whose congregation had consisted of two—a widow and her son.

Joseph's humiliating years in slavery and prison would not be the course some of us might choose as preparation for his future role as prime minister of a nation as huge as Egypt. But this was exactly the preparation God knew he needed.

Both Elijah and Joseph are, in a sense, like Christ, of whom the writer of Hebrews said: "Though he were a Son, yet learned he obedience by the things which he suffered" (Heb. 5:8).

The parallel in Joseph's life with the life of Jesus is too obvious to miss. Both were greatly loved by their fathers. Both were sent on a mission to find their brothers—Joseph to the other sons of Jacob, and Jesus to the lost of the world.

Both Joseph and Jesus were hated by their brothers without due cause. Both were plotted against, stripped of their robes, sold for the price of a slave, bound, rejected, falsely accused.

And both were highly exalted. When Joseph rode through the streets of Egypt, the people were commanded to "Bow the knee" (Gen. 41:43). Paul, in speaking of the exalted Christ, said the day would come when "every knee should bow, of things in heaven, and things in earth, and things under the earth; and that every tongue should confess that Jesus Christ is Lord, to the glory of God the Father" (Phil. 2:10, 11).

The glory of exaltation comes at the price of suffering. Peter wrote: "But the God of all grace, who hath called us unto his eternal glory by Christ Jesus, after that ye have suffered a while, make you perfect, stablish, strengthen, settle you" (1 Pet. 5:10).

God's purpose in Joseph's suffering was to prepare him for rulership over all the land of Egypt, second only to Pharaoh himself. What an amazing turn of events—from prisoner to prime minister!

LESSONS FROM JOSEPH

The Apostle Paul gave us a key to the Old Testament regarding what we may learn from these Old Testament men and women: "Now all these things happened unto them for ensamples: and they are written for our admonition, upon whom the ends of the world are come" (1 Cor. 10:11). This being true, what are some of the lessons we might draw from the life and suffering of Joseph?

Don't try to understand all the reasons for suffering. All
that Joseph had to support him, to trust in, during his
slavery and imprisonment were the dreams he had as a
boy in his father's home. It would have taken a direct
revelation from God to help a young man like Joseph to
understand that being sold into slavery by his brothers,
being falsely accused by his master's wife, being
forgotten by the fellow prisoner for so long—that all
these things had a good purpose.

It seems that Joseph himself didn't fully understand
why it had all happened until he saw his brothers and
father safely established in the grasslands of Egypt,
while the rest of the world languished in worldwide
famine. God had sent him to Egypt ahead of his family
in order that he might not only save his family but also
the land of Egypt. Egypt has always been equated with
evil, but we must remember that on several occasions
Egypt provided a safe haven for the people of God: for
Abraham during a famine, for Israel in the time of
famine in Joseph's time, and for the baby Jesus in the
time of the wicked Herods of Israel.

We must emphasize again how important it is for
Christians to realize that some of the suffering in this
world will not be fully understood until later. So often
believers grope in darkness and desperation, trying with
no success to explain some severe tragedy in their lives,
a struggle that brings no answers and increases the
frustration.

After the funeral of an only child, a teenage son, the
heartbroken parents might conclude: "Well, at least now
we know just why God allowed Bobby to be killed on
his bike. Three of his buddies received Christ during
the funeral service."

Please don't misunderstand. This result may well be

part of the reason for Bobby's death. But it will probably occur to the grieving parents that other teenagers can respond to the invitation to receive Christ in a regular church service without the death of a friend on his bike! To rack one's brain to justify every tragedy is unrealistic in terms of what we already know about God.

First, we know that God never makes a mistake, so we know that he has a specific reason for the suffering, which will someday come to light. Sometimes we can see part of the reason, as in the case of this teenage boy.

We know also that someday all the reasons behind the ordeals we face will be clear to us. We can conclude, with Paul, that all things, even the death of a loved one, work together for God's glory and our ultimate good.

Compare present suffering with coming glory. Paul wrote, "For I reckon that the sufferings of this present time are not worthy to be compared with the glory which shall be revealed in us" (Rom. 8:18).

It is possible to take a lump of black coal and transform this relatively worthless object into a glittering diamond of priceless value. Let us imagine for a moment that the lump of coal could think, talk, plan, feel, and decide for itself. Upon knowing the facts involved, do you think it would subject itself to such a transformation? I surely think that it would. I believe it would count the fiery heat and awful pressure as nothing compared to the diamond nature which awaited it.

So it should be within us. Jesus stressed this concept of allowing the prize awaiting us to interpret the pain, using an analogy of childbirth: "Verily, verily, I say unto you, That ye shall weep and lament, but the world shall rejoice: and ye shall be sorrowful, but your sorrow shall be turned into joy. A woman when she is in travail hath sorrow, because her hour is come: but as soon as she is delivered of the child, she remembereth no more the anguish, for joy that a man is born into the world" (John 16:20, 21).

John Chrysostom rightly understood this principle. When this staunch believer was brought before the Roman emperor in the fifth century and threatened with banishment for his faith, he replied, "Thou canst not banish me, for this world is my Father's house."

"But I will slay thee," said the emperor.

"Nay, thou canst not," said the noble champion, "for my life is hid with Christ in God."

"I will take away thy treasures."

"Nay, but thou canst not, for my treasure is in heaven and my heart is there."

"But I will drive thee away from man and thou shalt have no friend left."

"Nay, but thou canst not, for I have a friend in heaven from whom thou canst not separate me! I defy thee; for there is nothing that thou canst do to hurt me!"

Perhaps in the mercy of God, Joseph did know something of what would result from the suffering he underwent, but we can't be sure. We know that others in the Scriptures underwent hardship because they believed that God was working their circumstances for their ultimate good. Of Abraham it was said, "when he was called to go out into a place which he should after receive for an inheritance, obeyed: and he went out, not

knowing whither he went" (Heb. 11:8). We are left to
believe that Joseph's faith in God was so strong that he
accepted what was happening to him as something
God was allowing. Believing as he did in God, he must
have believed also that God had some greater good to
accomplish through it, as Joseph later came to
understand: "For God did send me before you to
preserve life" (Gen. 45:5), and "to preserve you a
posterity in the earth, and to save your lives by a great
deliverance" (Gen. 45:7).

Thank God for it. We know that we have gone full circle
with suffering when we come to the place where we
can thank God for what he has accomplished through
it. We see this sentiment in Joseph's remarks to his
brothers, when he realized fully that his coming to
Egypt as he did was the only possible way he could
have arrived at such a position of usefulness to preserve
them all from death.

Though it may come as a harsh-sounding exhortation
when we are in the midst of suffering, I believe God
wants us to thank him for the difficult time, even when
we don't yet see the reasons for it. The Psalmist wrote:
"Why art thou cast down, O my soul? and why art
thou disquieted in me? hope thou in God: for I shall yet
praise him for the help of his countenance" (Ps. 42:5).

Our church at Thomas Road has one of the largest
weekly prayer meetings in the nation. Each Wednesday
night some 1,500 to 2,000 small groups of two or three
people assemble and pray together during the service.
Their prayers, like yours and mine, are filled with both
petitions and praise. How good it is to hear believers
praying: "Lord, I want to thank you for healing my

mother," or "Thank you, dear Father, for my wonderful wife," or "To God be the glory, you provided money and my debt is paid."

But I wonder just how many of their prayers—and yours and mine—include the following thoughts: "Lord, I want to thank you for my illness," or "Praise God for this staggering financial problem which has suddenly come into my life."

"Wait a minute!" someone might say. "Are you really expected to thank God for these terrible things?" Let Paul answer the question for us: "In every thing give thanks: for this is the will of God in Christ Jesus concerning you" (1 Thess. 5:18).

When we are undergoing difficulties, I believe God expects us to ask him to remove these burdens. But even amidst the trouble and tragedy, we are to praise and thank him for entrusting us with the suffering and for allowing us to grow through it. A good rule to observe is: "Be careful for nothing, be prayerful in everything, be thankful for everything."

CHAPTER FOUR

Job the Sufferer

JOB is usually the first Bible character we think about when someone mentions suffering. It is doubtful whether any other human being suffered more than did this patriarch. In less than twenty-four hours this rich, influential, godly, family man literally saw his entire world collapse before his eyes.

First he lost his immense wealth. During a raid by a band of Sabeans, his oxen and donkeys were stolen and his herdsmen killed. Then his sheep and shepherds were destroyed by a fire which came from heaven, perhaps lightning or a meteorite. A few hours later his camels were stolen and his servants killed during a Chaldean raid.

While this was happening, Job's seven sons and three daughters were together feasting. Suddenly a windstorm struck the house and all of his ten children were killed. Since Job's was a very closely-knit family, the loss of his children must have devastated him. Job had spent many hours praying for his children and making sacrifices to the Lord on their behalf. While still reeling from the loss of all his wealth, he had to spend the rest of the day preparing the funerals for his ten children.

Satan's third attack took away Job's health. Some

think he had elephantiasis, a form of leprosy. Others think it was a form of leukemia of the skin. Whatever his ailments were, his whole body was covered with oozing boils, causing him excruciating pain. His skin became crusty and hard (Job 7:5). His agony was so great it seemed to pierce his bones (30:17), a feeling to which many who have had overwhelming infections can testify. His discomfort was intensified by a burning fever (30:30).

His suffering went beyond the physical and emotional. Because Job lost his family and wealth, he lost also his reputation. At first his friends and neighbors were sympathetic, but eventually they began to believe that Job was suffering because of some terrible secret sin. This loss of reputation seemed to be on Job's mind as much as his physical suffering. He said, "He [God] hath put my brethren far from me, and mine acquaintance are verily estranged from me" (19:13). In another place he cried, "My kinsfolk have failed, and my familiar friends have forgotten me" (19:14).

The loss of the respect of friends and servants was painful to Job: "I called my servant, but he gave me no answer" (19:16), and "All my inward friends abhorred me: and they whom I loved are turned against me (19:19). It seems the only thing worse than suffering is the feeling that one is suffering alone.

During his troubles, Job also lost the support of his wife. If ever a man needed the prayers and comfort of a godly wife, it was Job at this time in his life. Yet, the only advice this woman had for him was to curse God and die (2:9). One might wonder if this was the reason Satan didn't take Job's wife also, knowing she, rather than being supportive, would be part of his problem.

SUFFERING WITH JOB

The Book of Job becomes a roadmap for us as we identify with his experiences. Unlike Joseph, Job's reaction to his problems was mixed.

His first reaction was commendable. Immediately upon hearing of the loss of his wealth and his children we read: "Then Job arose, and rent his mantle, and shaved his head, and fell down upon the ground, and worshipped, and said, Naked came I out of my mother's womb, and naked shall I return thither: the Lord gave, and the Lord hath taken away; blessed be the name of the Lord. In all this Job sinned not, nor charged God foolishly" (Job 1:20-22).

But later Job became despondent. "After this opened Job his mouth, and cursed his day. And Job spake, and said, Let the day perish wherein I was born, and the night in which it was said, There is a man child conceived. . . . Why died I not from the womb? why did I not give up the ghost when I came out of the belly?" (Job 3:1-3, 11).

Job then began to blame God for his problems. "If I had called, and he had answered me; yet would I not believe that he had hearkened unto my voice. For he breaketh me with a tempest, and multiplieth my wounds without cause. He will not suffer me to take my breath, but filleth me with bitterness. . . . If the scourge slay suddenly, he will laugh at the trial of the innocent" (9:16-18, 23).

In his book, *The Suffering God,* Charles Ohlrich tells us: "In 1960, after four intensely happy years of marriage, C. S. Lewis's wife, Joy, died of cancer. In an effort to assuage his grief and guard against losing his

faith, Lewis wrote a journal in which he openly
expressed his feelings and doubts. A few years later the
journal was published under the title, *A Grief Observed*.
In the early pages, Lewis writes, 'Not that I am . . . in
much danger of ceasing to believe in God. The real
danger is coming to believe such dreadful things about
Him. The conclusion I dread is not, So there's no God
after all, but, So this is what God is really like. Deceive
yourself no longer.' "

*Job then longed for "the good old days" when he enjoyed
both riches and respect.* "Oh that I were as in months
past, as in the days when God preserved me; when his
candle shined upon my head, and when by his light I
walked through darkness; as I was in the days of
my youth, when the secret of God was upon my
tabernacle; when the Almighty was yet with me, when
my children were about me; . . . when I went out to the
gate through the city, when I prepared my seat in the
street! The young men saw me, and hid themselves: and
the aged arose, and stood up. The princes refrained
talking, and laid their hand on their mouth. The nobles
held their peace, and their tongue cleaved to the roof of
their mouth" (29:2-5, 7-10).

*Job seemed for the moment to hold onto his belief that his
suffering was unfair.* He felt he had deserved God's
blessing and that the respect others showed him was
well deserved, earned by his many good works.
"Because I delivered the poor that cried, and the
fatherless, and him that had none to help him. The
blessing of him that was ready to perish came upon
me: and I caused the widow's heart to sing for joy. . . . I
was eyes to the blind, and feet was I to the lame. I was

a father to the poor: and the cause which I knew not I searched out. And I brake the jaws of the wicked, and plucked the spoil out of his teeth" (29:12, 13, 15-17).

Job's confusion continued because he felt that God had rewarded such good deeds with a good life and a good ending. "Then I said, I shall die in my nest, and I shall multiply my days as the sand. My root was spread out by the waters, and the dew lay all night upon my branch. My glory was fresh in me, and my bow was renewed in my hand" (29:18-20).

Many of us who suffer have the same thoughts as Job did. But most important, we must work through our sorrow to the conclusions that Job found. In spite of his pain, and the fact that he didn't understand the reason for his suffering, he said, "Though he slay me, yet will I trust him . . ." (Job 13:15).

Job realized that in spite of his earthly suffering there lay ahead better prospects: "For I know that my redeemer liveth, and that he shall stand at the latter day upon the earth: And though after my skin worms destroy this body, yet in my flesh shall I see God: Whom I shall see for myself, and mine eyes shall behold, and not another; though my reins be consumed within me" (19:25-27).

Suffering is a teacher. Two very special courses of study are offered in the school of suffering. The first lesson is dependence. For many Christians the most difficult statement to accept is "for without me ye can do nothing" (John 15:5). Sometimes we would prefer to depend on our own natural abilities, our education, our experience, our personality rather than depend on God. But in this passage Jesus was saying that unless he is in full control, then nothing we do will achieve eternal significance. At times the only way God can prove his point in our lives is to remove some of the crutches we depend on, forcing us to see how helpless we are and making it necessary for us to lean completely on him.

A little girl was introduced to a wealthy and successful businessman her father had invited home for dinner. He told her, "This is Mr. Bradley, and he's a self-made millionaire." After the guest had left, the little girl asked her father, "Daddy, if he's a self-made man, why did he make himself so ugly?"

Whether we want to accept it or not, there is no such thing as a spiritually successful man—only those who have learned to depend on God can be called spiritually successful.

Debbie, one of the students at Liberty Baptist was born with cerebral palsy. At that time everyone assumed that children born with her problem were mentally retarded, so very little was done to help her learn or develop.

Debbie often heard her mother say of a younger brother who had died at birth, "I'm so glad Scottie died; he would have been just like Debbie, and there is no way I could have handled two of them."

Everything seemed to be going against Debbie. Her father had a gambling problem, and one of her father's friends several times tried to abuse her sexually, saying, "Nobody else will love you, so I will." At least once a year Debbie's parents would have a big argument and threaten to get a divorce. She never knew if they would go through with it or not.

But when Debbie was fifteen, the Lord touched her life through a very loving, caring pastor, who encouraged her, even though her parents kept saying there was no hope for her. But that pastor moved on to another church, and the next pastor wouldn't allow

Debbie to do anything in the church, because he said it might "offend" people. When she thought of going off to a university, her pastor said, "Debbie, you'll never make it; you might as well forget it." Her parents' reaction was even worse.

She was the first seriously handicapped person to attend Liberty Baptist, so it was difficult. But she persisted, finally graduated, and is now working in one of the offices here at the college.

Again, we don't have the answer for why Debbie has had to suffer so much. But her answer was, "I heard an illustration that meant a lot to me. When a person is climbing up a mountain, and gets half way up, he can look and see how much farther he has to go. But the great thing is that he can look back and see how far he has come. Life is sometimes overwhelming, but knowing that there is so much more a merciful heavenly Father has to teach me keeps me going."

The second course taught in the school of suffering is obedience. The author of Psalm 119 wrote: "Before I was afflicted I went astray: but now have I kept thy word. . . . It is good for me that I have been afflicted; that I might learn thy statutes" (vv. 67, 71). Those who suffer for obedience's sake should not despair, but rather glory in it, for such sufferers are in good company. Our Lord himself benefited from this kind of suffering while on earth. "Though he were a Son, yet learned he obedience by the things which he suffered" (Heb. 5:8).

Suffering teaches us about ourselves. During one of Job's defenses against the false accusations of his three friends, he cried out: "My righteousness I hold fast, and will not let go: my heart shall not reproach me so long as I live" (Job 27:6). But as a result of his intense suffering and personal encounter with God, Job finally saw himself as he really was: "Wherefore I abhor myself, and repent in dust and ashes" (42:6).

This benefit of suffering is illustrated by Jesus in the parable of the prodigal son. In the story, a father's youngest son demanded his share of the family inheritance and left home to begin living a life of sin in another country. But all too soon his money was gone and with it his friends. In desperation, the boy agreed to tend someone's hogs, something a Jew would consider utterly repulsive. To prevent starvation, the young man actually ate with the pigs. One of the key lessons of this parable is found in Luke 15:17, "And when he came to himself. . . ." Perhaps his wise and loving father had already anticipated this would happen, which would explain why he gave his son the inheritance with no argument. All his advice against his son's leaving home would have been futile until the headstrong boy "came to himself." And what a difference this made! Note the son's remarks on reaching this point: "I will arise and go to my father, and will say unto him, Father, I have sinned against heaven, and before thee" (Luke 15:18).

This parable was told to illustrate a lost sinner finding God, and of Israel's attitude toward God's offer of grace to repentant Gentiles, but I'm convinced it illustrates how a wayward son coming back to his heavenly Father first learns something of himself from the bad experience. A clear benefit of suffering is that it can cause us to "come to ourselves."

Suffering gives insight into God's person. After Job had suffered he was able to say, "I have heard of thee by the hearing of the ear, but now mine eye seeth thee" (Job

42:5). Job's pain had allowed him to understand spiritual truths which could not otherwise have been learned.

Pain may help us understand a mystery such as the one we read about in the Book of Hosea. God gave Hosea the strange command to marry a harlot. "Go, take unto thee a wife of whoredoms and children of whoredoms: for the land hath committed great whoredom, departing from the Lord. So he went and took Gomer the daughter of Diblaim; which conceived, and bare him a son" (Hosea 1:2, 3).

To understand why God would issue such an order to Hosea, some historical background is needed. In Hosea's day, some seven centuries before Christ, the nation Israel had abandoned the true God for the false idols of the pagan tribes around them. This unfaithfulness both angered and grieved the Lord, for he considered himself the husband of that nation, and her idolatries as adultery. God ordered Hosea to marry an unfaithful woman so that the prophet could understand in some small degree how offensive Israel's spiritual unfaithfulness was to her injured husband. Hosea's insight into God's feelings was perhaps unknown by any other Old Testament prophet—insight gained only through suffering.

During the Lord's suffering in the Garden of Gethsemane, he cried out, "Abba, Father, all things are possible unto thee; take away this cup from me: nevertheless not what I will, but what thou wilt" (Mark 14:36). This word "Abba" is an Aramaic term, expressing a special familiarity and intimacy between a father and his child. The closest English translation is "Dear pappa," or "Beloved daddy." This reference to God as "Abba" is found but three times in the New

Testament, and on two occasions it is connected with suffering. The reference above was to Christ's suffering. Paul spoke of the believer suffering: "Ye have received the Spirit of adoption, whereby we cry, Abba, Father. . . . If so be that we suffer with him, that we may be also glorified together. For I reckon that the sufferings of this present time are not worthy to be compared with the glory which shall be revealed in us" (Rom. 8:15, 17, 18). Intimacy with God is gained through suffering.

Suffering silences the devil. One of the most dramatic confrontations of all time was between God and Satan, described in the Book of Job. Satan arrogantly stood before the Almighty and claimed that the only reason Job served God was due to all the material benefits which accompanied such service. Note his accusation: "Doth Job fear God for nought? Hast not thou made an hedge about him, and about his house, and about all that he hath on every side? thou hast blessed the work of his hands, and his substance is increased in the land. But put forth thine hand now, and touch all that he hath, and he will curse thee to thy face" (Job 1:9, 10, 11).

Were these terrible charges valid? Would Job defect under persecution? The sovereign and all-knowing God, of course, needed no such assurance. But to silence the devil, to utterly disprove his vicious and unfounded taunts, God allowed Satan to persecute Job.

Perhaps you are reading these very lines, undergoing an especially difficult experience. As the pain grows, you begin to wonder why God is allowing it. What have I done to deserve this? you ask.

Is it possible that God is pointing you out to Satan as

he once did Job? God was proud of his faithful servant. Notice how God talked about him: "And the Lord said unto Satan, Hast thou considered my servant Job, that there is none like him in the earth, a perfect and an upright man, one that feareth God, and escheweth evil?" (Job 1:8). God might be proud of you and your service for Christ, and Satan is saying, "Why shouldn't he (she) serve you? You offer the best fringe benefits in town—good health, work at a well-paying job, a nice home, a nice car, and some extra money in the bank. But just let me move in and take some of those goodies from him (her) and he (she) will turn away from you."

God wants to say to Satan concerning you: "Go ahead and do your worst—but only up to a certain point. You'll soon learn what I already know, that my child loves me for who I am, and not because of certain material things I've given him (her)." Remembering what we know about God, if he does allow something like this to happen, he has already provided grace sufficient for us, so that we can stand in the time of temptation (1 Cor. 10:13).

LESSONS FROM JOB

If Job's suffering had been for him alone, his story might never have been retold in the Scriptures. God obviously wanted us to learn from Job's suffering, just why it was permitted, and how we are to react when we suffer.

Don't despise suffering. At first glance, Hebrews 12:5 seems to offer strange advice: "My son, despise not thou the chastening of the Lord, nor faint when thou art rebuked of him." To despise simply means "to count as nothing." We use the word today to express hate or abhorrence of something or someone. The biblical term *despise* refers to "lightly dismissing something as unimportant." In this same chapter (Heb. 12:16), we are given the example of Esau who despised his birthright. Esau didn't hate it. To him it was simply unimportant and trivial, so he eagerly traded it for a bowl of soup. All this is to say that we are not to take God's chastening lightly.

In the Old Testament, Lot, nephew of Abraham, is an example of someone who despised chastening. When an argument arose between Lot's and Abraham's herdsmen over grazing rights, Abraham, to avoid trouble, allowed Lot to choose the land he wanted and Abraham agreed to take what was left. "Then Lot chose him all the plain of Jordan; and Lot journeyed east: and they separated themselves the one from the other. Abram dwelled in the land of Canaan, and Lot dwelled in the cities of the plain, and pitched his tent toward Sodom" (Gen. 13:11, 12).

Soon Lot had actually moved into the city itself. When Sodom became involved in a losing war, a number of the leading citizens of the city, including Lot, were carried off into slavery by the victorious army. Upon hearing the news, Abraham gathered his forces of trained servants and defeated the marauding army north of the Sea of Galilee. Lot was set free.

This episode doesn't seem to be an accident, but something God had permitted to chasten and correct Lot for living among the people of Sodom. But now the lesson was over. Lot was free, and given another chance. However, he went right back to Sodom, apparently learning nothing from his ordeal. Finally, when the perversions of Sodom had become intolerable,

God decided to destroy the city. Lot was not only still living there but had allowed his daughters to marry men of Sodom. The tragic account ends, and Lot escaped, of course, along with his wife and two unmarried daughters. But the married girls died in the flames. Just outside the burning city, Lot's wife was also struck dead for her sin. His two daughters, fearing they would go childless, made their father drunk and caused him to commit incest with them. The last glimpse we have of Lot, he is huddled in a gloomy cave, cold and miserable, tormented, no doubt, by the awful guilt of his sin.

God deals with us as with children. He deals in love. Even his chastenings are for the purpose of turning us away from the sins that would bring us even more harm. When we neglect to learn from the chastening he sends, we open ourselves up to the possibility of even more severe punishment. Lot learned that lesson too late.

Expect suffering. If no suffering ever comes our way, we should be surprised—perhaps even worried. Paul wrote to Timothy: "All that will live godly in Christ Jesus shall suffer persecution" (2 Tim. 3:12).

God loves us too much to keep us from suffering. There seems to be an immutable law in the universe that says certain lessons concerning ourselves, our world, and our God can only be learned in the school of suffering. Thus, the heavenly Father, like any concerned earthly father, desires the best education for his sons and daughters.

The writer of Hebrews spoke of this: "Furthermore we have had fathers of our flesh which corrected us, and we gave them reverence: shall we not much rather

be in subjection unto the Father of spirits, and live? For
they verily for a few days chastened us after their own
pleasure; but he for our profit, that we might be
partakers of his holiness" (Heb. 12:9, 10).

Obviously, some suffering comes as a result of our
own sins and failures. But much of it is inherent in our
trying to live the Christian life. Jesus was concerned
about his disciples, knowing that they would face many
difficult situations because of their love for him. "If ye
were of the world, the world would love his own: but
because ye are not of the world, but I have chosen you
out of the world, therefore the world hateth you.
Remember the word that I said unto you, The servant is
not greater than his lord. If they have persecuted me,
they will also persecute you; if they have kept my
sayings, they will keep yours also" (John 15:19, 20).

Later Jesus told them: "They shall put you out of the
synagogues: yea, the time cometh, that whosoever
killeth you will think that he doeth God service. . . .
Verily, verily, I say unto you, That ye shall weep and
lament, but the world shall rejoice: and ye shall be
sorrowful, but your sorrow shall be turned into joy"
(John 16:2, 20).

So in the midst of suffering, the proper response
should not be Why? but rather Why not? We should
enjoy the sunlight but expect the storms also, and
always be careful to thank God for both. Remember
Jesus' last words to his disciples: "These things I have
spoken unto you, that in me ye might have peace. In
the world ye shall have tribulation: but be of good
cheer; I have overcome the world" (John 16:33).

Don't faint because of suffering. It is just as bad to treat
suffering too seriously as to regard it too lightly. The

truth is that we sometimes overreact to God's chastisement. God's Word is clear: "My son, despise not thou the chastening of the Lord, nor faint when thou art rebuked of him" (Heb. 12:5).

A young man graduated from our school several years ago and answered the call of God to preach. According to his professors, he had an ability to preach that is rarely seen in men his age. Upon graduation he moved to another state and started a new church. For a while things went well. His church grew numerically and spiritually. But then he made some unwise decisions and ran into trouble, possibly due to his lack of experience or immaturity. Eventually God brought some gentle rebukes his way, but he wasn't able to take it. He was so shocked and hurt that he left the church, returned to his old secular job, and hasn't preached since.

How sad! This young man is now frustrated and embittered, and unless a drastic change comes, he'll spend his remaining years not using the gifts God has given him. The writer of Proverbs said, "If thou faint in the day of adversity, thy strength is small" (Prov. 24:10).

Paul gave the challenge "And let us not be weary in well doing: for in due season we shall reap, if we faint not" (Gal. 6:9). D. L. Moody used to say that God could never use a discouraged Christian. It has been my experience that God does not determine a man's greatness by his wealth or his education but by how much or how little it takes to discourage him.

One of our students had some unusual problems to face. Many people in his condition would have given up long ago, but Brad Schaaf doesn't give up.

Brad was born deaf, and spent several years in a school for the deaf before he came to Liberty Baptist

College. The transition wasn't easy for him. He had a difficult time when he suspected roommates were talking about him when he couldn't see their faces to read what they were saying. It would have been easy for him to excuse himself and his own behavior, since he hadn't been used to living with hearing people. But through these difficult times he allowed some good things to happen. Through the problems, he allowed God to show him lessons he needed to learn about pride and self-sufficiency. Rather than becoming bitter, he allowed the difficulties to make him better.

Someone once reminded us that life on earth is difficult, and the sooner we realize this and accept it as fact, the easier life can become for us. If we expect to escape suffering, we will always be disappointed. All of life involves suffering somewhere along the line. The secret is to learn, like Job, that God has purposes for it, and we can profit from it when we accept it and learn the lessons it brings.

CHAPTER FIVE

Jeremiah
the Sufferer

JEREMIAH, like Job, experienced pain and persecution as few of us ever will. The terrible things which befell him remind us of stories of the ancient torture chambers within medieval castles in Europe.

Jeremiah's Book of Lamentations amounts to a funeral dirge over the twisted bodies and crumbling buildings of Jerusalem after Nebuchadnezzar's final attack. The prophet made two revealing statements about his experiences of life: "I am a man that hath seen affliction" (Lam. 3:1). In the opening verses he asked, "Behold, and see if there be any sorrow like unto my sorrow, which is done unto me, wherewith the Lord hath afflicted me in the day of his fierce anger" (Lam. 1:12).

God called Jeremiah to preach some very unpopular messages about sin and the resulting judgment that would come to Jerusalem. Jeremiah said that God would judge Judah by sending Nebuchadnezzar against them. Because of Jeremiah's fearless sermons, he was made to suffer many things.

His messages made him so unpopular that people from his own hometown plotted to kill him, and even his own family turned against him. Even those who

claimed to be the religious leaders rejected him.
Pashhur, the chief temple priest, had him whipped and
put in stocks. A wild mob of priests and prophets
nearly killed him. Hananiah, a false prophet, ridiculed
him. King Jehoiakim of Judah threatened his life. Later
he was arrested and imprisoned, charged with treason.
On one occasion a group of hotheads placed him in an
empty cistern in the prison yard, leaving him to sink
down into the mire.

More serious and painful perhaps than the physical
abuse was seeing the original manuscript of his
prophecy burned by King Jehoiakim. Perhaps twenty
years of his work went up in smoke. Jewish leaders,
refusing to listen to his warnings, forced him to
accompany them to Egypt where, according to tradition,
he died lonely and desolate. With good reason Jeremiah
was called the weeping prophet, for through his tears
we see a brokenhearted God, who was pained when his
message to his people was rejected.

How does one react when pain and sorrow keep
coming, wave after wave, as it did to Jeremiah? We
have seen friends go through such periods.

Several years ago Dr. and Mrs. Rudy Holland took
their young son Paul for an eye examination when they
discovered that his eyes were not dilating properly. A
short time later extensive tests showed that Paul had a
brain tumor.

Surgery was performed to remove the tumor, but
eleven months later the family received the dis-
heartening news that the tumor had returned, this
time much larger and inoperable. They were told that
little Paul had less than a year to live.

New hope was awakened when they heard that a
new technique had been developed at Boston Children's

Hospital to help patients such as Paul. Because of complications that arose while undergoing treatment in Boston, Paul had to have further surgery to relieve the innercranial pressure building up as a result of the increasing size of the tumor.

After many months of watching Paul suffer, the Hollands were able to take him home. There he began to return, more or less, to normal. But he was being kept alive with synthetic hormones, since his pituitary gland had been destroyed by the growing tumor.

On a family picnic some months later, a cyst that had formed in connection with the brain tumor ruptured and soon Paul was back in the hospital in a coma where he remained for thirty-two days. A month later he lapsed into another thirty-two-day coma. The family was told that Paul had lost all of his body functions, that his memory had been erased by the rupturing cyst, and that he would be blind.

Over the years, Paul regained some of his body functions: he can feed himself, he knows his parents, but he has very little memory.

Paul's older sister, Angie, described it well in a question put to her father. "Daddy, Paul died instantly, didn't he?" referring to that moment when the cyst ruptured in his brain. Of course, Paul is still alive, but the personality of the little brother she had known was gone forever, as if he had actually died.

How can one put into words the kind of suffering and pain a family like the Hollands go through? When the hurt just keeps coming, and one trial after another sweeps in, month after month, a form of exhaustion sometimes sets in. Again, more important than the pain we feel are the lessons that can be learned from it, and what God sees our reactions to be.

SUFFERING WITH JEREMIAH

At first, Jeremiah's suffering brought negative responses, much as Job experienced. He began to talk back to God: "O Lord, thou has deceived me, and I was deceived: thou art stronger than I, and hast prevailed: I am in derision daily, every one mocketh me. For since I spake, I cried out, I cried violence and spoil; because the word of the Lord was made a reproach unto me, and a derision, daily. Then I said, I will not make mention of him, nor speak any more in his name. But his word was in mine heart as a burning fire shut up in my bones, and I was weary with forbearing, and I could not stay" (Jer. 20:7-9).

Like Job, Jeremiah began to wish he hadn't been born. In fact, his words sound almost identical to Job's. "Cursed be the day wherein I was born: let not the day wherein my mother bare me be blessed. Cursed be the man who brought tidings to my father, saying, A man child is born unto thee; making him very glad. And let that man be as the cities which the Lord overthrew, and repented not: and let him hear the cry in the morning, and the shouting at noontide; because he slew me not from the womb; or that my mother might have been my grave, and her womb to be always great with me. Wherefore came I forth out of the womb to see labour and sorrow, that my days should be consumed with shame?" (20:14-18; cf. Job 3:3-13).

Later Jeremiah began to think more positively about what he was undergoing: "This I recall to my mind, therefore have I hope. It is of the Lord's mercies that we are not consumed, because his compassions fail not. They are new every morning: great is thy faithfulness. The Lord is my portion, saith my soul; therefore will I hope in him. The Lord is good unto them that wait for him, to the soul that seeketh him. It is good that a man should both hope and quietly wait for the salvation of the Lord" (Lam. 3:21-26).

Even those who suffer deeply can keep a proper perspective concerning the Lord and his purposes: "For the Lord will not cast off for ever: But though he cause grief, yet will he have compassion according to the multitude of his mercies. For he doth not afflict willingly nor grieve the children of men" (Lam. 3:31-33).

LESSONS FROM JEREMIAH

It is hard to read Jeremiah or Lamentations without sensing the deep pain the prophet felt for his countrymen, who refused to listen to God's Word of warning. It is hard to tell where his own personal pain left off and his suffering over his rejected messages began. It is also difficult sometimes to see where the cries of his own broken heart and God's broken heart left off and began. But from Jeremiah's suffering come lessons for us as we face painful experiences.

Suffering drives us closer to God. B. W. Woods, in his book, *Understanding Suffering* (Grand Rapids, Baker, 1974), gave an interesting observation from nature: "In the spring the roaming cattle in some hot countries are driven out of the swampy lowlands unto the higher hill country by the furious insects. In reality, the painful insects save the cattle from the diseases so prevalent among livestock in the fever-filled lowlands. The parallel is easily evident when applied to the part discipline and hardship play in Christian growth. Sometimes our sorrows drive us from the dangerous swamp lands of an easy life into the pure alpine air of God's higher purposes."

The Apostle Paul wrote: "Most gladly therefore will I rather glory in my infirmities, that the power of Christ may rest upon me" (2 Cor. 12:9).

Augustine once observed, "God wants to give us something but cannot, because our hands are full— there is no where for Him to put it."

During that awful April night in 1912 as the mighty Titanic was going down, carrying to their death more than 1500 passengers, the ship's band struck up a song to help cheer the doomed people. The song was the hymn "Nearer, My God, to Thee." If we don't learn any other lesson from suffering than that, we will have learned a very precious lesson. When Jeremiah was in the bottom of the cistern, there was nowhere to cast his eyes but straight up, to heaven. As Augustine suggested, sometimes God has to send suffering to take everything else out of our hands so he can fill it with the good things he desires us to have.

Suffering makes us like Christ. Years ago, during his first semester at Bible college, one of my associates here at Thomas Road Baptist Church purchased a little wall plaque which bore a verse from Philippians. It read, "That I may know him, and the power of his resurrection." He was always inspired by the verse, since it was the first thing he saw every morning as he got out of bed. In fact, he decided to make it his life verse. One day a friend came into his room, saw the plaque, and reminded him that the entire verse was not printed on it. Embarrassed, he turned to his Bible to find what had been left off. Missing from the verse were the words: ". . . and the fellowship of his sufferings, being made conformable unto his death" (Phil. 3:10). According to this verse, one does not really get to know Christ until he enters into the fellowship of Christ's suffering and death. We want the power of the resurrection, but would prefer to leave off the suffering, and that is impossible. We simply can't have the one without the other.

Suffering calls us to pray. The Psalmist wrote, "And call upon me in the day of trouble: I will deliver thee, and thou shalt glorify me" (Ps. 50:15).

Usually, suffering will by its very nature increase our prayer time. But sometimes it can work the other way. If we become angry with God or doubt his ability to help us, we may be tempted to give up.

A statement in the Book of Job is very enlightening concerning suffering and prayer: "And the Lord turned the captivity of Job, when he prayed for his friends: also the Lord gave Job twice as much as he had before" (Job 42:10).

In the midst of Jeremiah's stress, he turned his eyes and his prayers to God. Unlike Jeremiah, sometimes in the midst of our pain it is hard to trust God for answers. When a father brought his child to Jesus to be healed, he said, "Lord, I believe; help thou mine unbelief" (Mark 9:24). In effect, this man was saying, "Lord, I know you demand a certain amount of faith to heal my son. I want you to know I'm trying as hard as I can to come up with the necessary faith. But it probably won't be enough. Therefore, will you take it from here and heal my son?"

When our faith seems to be the least is when we

should pray the most, regardless of how we feel. God rewards us on the basis of our faithfulness—not our feelings.

Suffering challenges us to commit ourselves to God. A story in the Old Testament comes to us as a clear example of what it means to commit ourselves to God in the face of suffering. Daniel's three friends, Shadrach, Meshach, and Abednego, were not teenagers, as some believe, but young men well established in Babylonian political life. At the beginning of their careers, with their whole lives ahead of them, they risked it all for the cause of standing true to their beliefs. If God could not take care of them at that point, then serving him in the future was futile. They answered Nebuchadnezzar, who was threatening to put them into a furnace, "If it be so, our God whom we serve is able to deliver us from the burning fiery furnace, and he will deliver us out of thine hand, O king. But if not, be it known unto thee, O king, that we will not serve thy gods, nor worship the golden image which thou hast set up" (Dan. 3:17, 18).

Where did this kind of courage and conviction come from? It stemmed from the fact that these three men had previously committed their souls to God. If our souls are committed to God from the beginning, the suffering we are called to bear becomes easier to accept and to endure.

I wonder what would have happened to Rudy Holland and his family had their eyes not been on the Lord during the time their son Paul was stricken with the brain tumor which caused the extensive brain damage. Because their eyes were on the Lord, he was able to teach them many things through the experience.

Some time ago, Rudy Holland shared five important lessons the Lord taught him. He has allowed me to share that part of a message he gave at that time.

The first lesson concerned *"God's unfailing grace.* I confess that there have been times when I did not feel I could go on," he said. "When I thought I would literally go to pieces, at that moment the grace of God would lift me and restore me and give strength for one more day. I wish I could explain to you how it occurs, but it is beyond human expression. When you have cried till you can cry no more, when you have hurt till you feel you can hurt no more, all seems to be lost, and then, all of a sudden, the burden seems lighter, a smile creeps across your face, hope surges through your soul with no apparent reason except that faith in God and his unfailing grace has enabled you once more to overcome the Tempter."

The second lesson was, as Rudy stated it, "I have learned of *God's inexhaustible supply.* God never guides where he does not provide. His way may seem hard, but along the way he has resting places and oases for refreshment."

The third lesson was *"God's unquestionable purpose.* Surely you would not be so naive as to think that Doris and I have not had our moments to question, 'Why, Lord?' I look around me and see other families who think only in terms of physical and financial or perhaps social success for their children. All we asked was that God would use our children for his service. Our daughter Angie, since she was six, has said, 'I want to be a missionary.' Paul, from the time he was five, said that he wanted to be a preacher. So we ask, 'Why our little boy, God—look at all those who could care less about your work?' Although I have no answers, I know

that God has an unquestionable purpose. Whatever it
is, I know that eventually it will be 'for good' and that
it will bring glory to God. Many times when Satan
brings up matters that will hinder us, we know that
God can turn it around and help us through it."

The fourth lesson concerned *"God's unexplainable
peace.* I cannot say I have had that peace from the
beginning. It was not until I had mentally 'buried' my
son, until I had given him completely to God, that the
peace came. We all say we have given our children to
God, but sometimes we haven't really given them up
until we sense that he has asked us for them in a way
we have not anticipated. I am reminded of Abraham
and Isaac, whom God asked to be slain on the altar of
sacrifice. When Abraham showed his willingness to go
through with it, God saw that Abraham had really
given up his son."

The fifth lesson was *"Learning to expect an
unpredictable result.* When our son Paul was really
feeling sick, he would sing to himself. The day we
found out that Paul had to have more surgery, his
grandparents came to visit us. They had promised him
a toy, a 'Big Wheel,' for his birthday. His grandfather
promised that he would help Paul put the toy together. I
can still remember seeing him, working away, heaving
with nausea, with severe headaches, losing the use of
his right side. Later that day, he asked if 'Nannie,' his
grandmother, could stay with him that night and, of
course, she did. As Paul was sitting with her on the
bed, still heaving with nausea, he asked, 'Nannie, why
does Jesus let me be so sick?' She answered that she
didn't know. Paul, between the heaves, began to sing,
'Jesus loves me, this I know, for the Bible tells me so.'

"Many days, coming back from his treatments in

Boston, Paul would be so sick he could hardly hold his head up. But as we would be driving down Memorial Avenue by the Charles River I could hear Paul singing, 'Amazing grace, how sweet the sound.' "

A story was told of a history professor who had been lecturing on a series of wars fought between the French and English several centuries ago. A student asked him, "Why is it that, almost without exception, the English won all those wars?"

The professor answered, "It was not because the English had bigger armies, braver soldiers, better equipment, or smarter generals. They won simply because they learned how to hang on a day longer."

The lessons about suffering are often difficult, especially those that Rudy and Doris Holland have had to learn through watching their son. But I wonder how anyone who had not committed his life to God, as they had done, could endure. I'm glad they are finding their answers from God, holding on to him, day by day.

CHAPTER SIX

Paul
the Sufferer

87

WE don't usually think of Paul as a sufferer. Paul
the great theological mind behind the Epistle to the
Romans, Paul the church planter, Paul the apostle to the
Gentile world, Paul the missionary—these are the roles
we usually associate with him.

When we examine the Scriptures, however, we see
that Paul's first presentation to the Christian church by
the Holy Spirit was given in terms of the suffering he
would have to endure.

The Lord spoke to Ananias of Damascus in a vision
telling him that a man named Saul would be found in
the house of Judas on a street called Straight. Ananias
knew Saul as one who had been persecuting the
church. To assure Ananias the Lord answered, "Go thy
way: for he [Saul] is a chosen vessel unto me, to bear
my name before the Gentiles, and kings, and the
children of Israel: For I will shew him how great things
he must suffer for my name's sake" (Acts 9:15, 16).

In a nutshell, these verses perfectly summarize Saul's
future life of service for Christ. He would indeed suffer
great things for the Lord's name. In fact, years later in a
Roman prison, Paul also spoke of it: "But what things
were gain to me, those I counted loss for Christ. Yea
doubtless, and I count all things but loss for the

excellency of the knowledge of Christ Jesus my Lord: for whom I have suffered the loss of all things, and do count them but dung, that I may win Christ" (Phil. 3:7, 8).

Paul may be thought of as the greatest Christian of all time. His amazing life can be summarized by four words: persecution, pain, performance, and praise. The first two words provided the root and soil from which sprang the fruit of performance and praise.

A list of his sufferings, physical and mental, sound like a catalog of torture. On numerous occasions he was plotted against, once in Damascus shortly after his conversion and several times in Jerusalem. On one such occasion, forty men vowed not to eat or drink until they had killed him.

Paul experienced long periods of distrust and dislike by other believers, and his work was constantly opposed by his countrymen. In Athens he was ridiculed, in Corinth he was falsely accused, on numerous occasions he was set upon by mobs of people.

Paul suffered physical abuse. He wrote of his sufferings: ". . . in labours more abundant, in stripes above measure, in prison more frequent, in deaths oft. Of the Jews five times received I forty stripes save one. Thrice was I beaten with rods, once was I stoned, thrice I suffered shipwreck, a night and a day I have been in the deep; in journeyings often, in perils of waters, in perils of robbers, in perils by mine own countrymen, in perils by the heathen, in perils in the city, in perils in the wilderness, in perils in the sea, in perils among false brethren; in weariness and painfulness, in watchings often, in hunger and thirst, in fastings often, in cold and nakedness" (2 Cor. 11:23-27).

Beyond this, Paul spoke of bearing responsibility of the gospel and the cares of others: "Beside those things that are without, that which cometh upon me daily, the care of all the churches. Who is weak, and I am not weak? who is offended, and I burn not? If I must needs glory, I will glory of the things which concern mine infirmities" (2 Cor. 11:28-30).

Paul knew the meaning of stress and internal pressure: "For we would not, brethren, have you ignorant of our trouble which came to us in Asia, that we were pressed out of measure, above strength, insomuch that we despaired even of life" (2 Cor. 1:8).

SUFFERING WITH PAUL

Perhaps Paul was not the greatest Christian who ever lived. But few would argue that he was the most widely used of God. One cannot help but believe that at least some of his usefulness was because of the exceptional manner in which he reacted to pain and persecution.

Paul accepted suffering because he knew that it had a purpose. When he was visiting in the house of Philip the evangelist at Caesarea, Paul was warned by the prophet Agabus that he should not go to Jerusalem. Paul's reply was: "I am ready not to be bound only, but also to die at Jerusalem for the name of the Lord Jesus" (Acts 21:13). He believed that his suffering would further the gospel in the same way that he felt God's grace to him would profit others.

Paul believed his suffering kept him trusting in God and not in his own self-sufficiency. Evidently Paul had some ongoing problem, probably physical, which he called "a thorn in the flesh, the messenger of Satan to buffet me, lest I should be exalted above measure" (2 Cor. 12:7). Paul prayed that the problem would be removed, but God chose instead to give him grace to bear it, which would keep him dependent on God for grace.

Paul took the long range view about suffering. Instead of wallowing in self-pity, he reveled in the reward that he knew would come someday if he remained faithful. To the Romans he wrote: "For I reckon that the sufferings of this present time are not worthy to be compared with the glory which shall be revealed in us" (Rom. 8:18). To the Corinthian church he wrote: "For our light affliction, which is but for a moment, worketh for us a far more exceeding and eternal weight of glory (2 Cor. 4:17).

Paul knew suffering produced fruit. Pain is the pruning of the branches so vital to the production of fruit. "Every branch in me [Christ] that beareth not fruit he taketh away: and every branch that beareth fruit, he purgeth it, that it may bring forth more fruit" (John 15:2). The Scriptures speak of a number of spiritual fruits produced through purging. Paul said it produced *patience.* "And not only so, but we glory in tribulations also: knowing that tribulation worketh patience" (Rom. 5:3). Suffering results in *joy.* "They that sow in tears shall reap in joy" (Ps. 126:5). It produces the fruit of *knowledge:* "Blessed is the man whom thou chastenest, O Lord, and teachest him out of thy law" (Ps. 94:12). We learn some things through prosperity, but we learn much more from adversity, for suffering produces the fruit of *maturity:* "Sorrow is better than laughter: for by the sadness of the countenance the heart is made better" (Eccles. 7:3). Peter wrote: "But the God of all grace, who hath called us unto his eternal glory by Christ Jesus, after that ye have suffered a while, make you perfect, stablish, strengthen, settle you" (1 Peter 5:10). During his farewell address to Israel, Moses reminded the people that one of God's purposes in allowing their discomfort in the wilderness was to make them mature people: "Who led thee through that great and terrible wilderness, wherein were fiery serpents, and scorpions, and drought, where there was no water . . . that he might humble thee, and that he might prove thee, to do thee good at thy latter end" (Deut. 8:15, 16). Suffering also produces the fruit of *righteousness*. "Now no chastening for the present seemeth to be joyous, but grievous: nevertheless afterward it yieldeth the peaceable fruit of right- eousness unto them which are exercised thereby" (Heb. 12:11). God allows us to suffer in order to make us *better* people, not *bitter* people.

Paul knew suffering qualified him to counsel and comfort others. He wrote, "Who comforteth us in all our tribulation, that we may be able to comfort them which are in any trouble, by the comfort wherewith we ourselves are comforted of God" (2 Cor. 1:4). His suffering, he felt, would help him comfort others. "For as the sufferings of Christ abound in us, so our consolation also aboundeth by Christ" (2 Cor. 1:5).

In effect, Paul was saying, "The more I suffer, the more God can comfort me, which allows me to be a faithful student. The more I suffer, the more I can comfort others, which allows me to become a faithful teacher." So, one who has suffered many things can then speak many languages. God does not comfort us to make us comfortable but to make us comforters.

Paul knew suffering furthered the gospel witness. On three different occasions Satan succeeded in having Paul cast into prison, trying to silence his witness for Christ. But just the opposite happened. In each case Paul was able to use his very prison cell as a platform to speak of the grace of God.

During Paul's second missionary journey, he and Silas were beaten and thrown into the jail in Philippi. But then a miracle happened. "At midnight Paul and Silas prayed, and sang praises unto God: and the prisoners heard them. And suddenly there was a great earthquake, so that the foundations of the prison were shaken: and immediately all the doors were opened, and every one's bands were loosed" (Acts 16:25, 26). The jailor, in fear, was ready to kill himself, but Paul stopped him. The jailor cried out, "Sirs, what must I do to be saved? And they said, Believe on the Lord Jesus Christ" (16:30, 31). From a beating and imprisonment came the beginning of the church in Philippi.

Later Paul was imprisoned in Rome. In his letter to this very church in Philippi, Paul wrote: "I would ye should understand, brethren, that the things which happened unto me have fallen out rather unto the furtherance of the gospel; so that my bonds in Christ are manifest in all the palace, and in all other places" (Phil. 1:12, 13).

During Paul's final imprisonment in Rome, he wrote to Timothy: "Notwithstanding the Lord stood with me, and strengthened me; that by me the preaching might be fully known, and that all the Gentiles might hear: and I was delivered out of the mouth of the lion" (2 Tim. 4:17).

Paul knew suffering made him an example for others. Few will disagree that in trying to influence others, an ounce of example is more effective than a pound of preaching. Some things about God's grace seem better "caught" than taught.

In his book, *Understanding Suffering*, B. W. Woods speaks of a missionary who lost his wife and child to disease:

The natives to whom he had preached watched his every move. They saw him walk to the grave in a quiet and stately manner. They sensed in his grief a note of hope and victory. One was heard to say, "I do not know about his religion, or about the Christ he serves, but I do know that I like the way he buries his dead. There is a difference in his sorrow and ours. We shriek with horror and anguish. We have no hope. This man acts as if he knows where his dead loved ones are going."

In the same way, the Apostle Paul was often better able to convey more spiritual truth about the all-sufficiency of Christ through his sufferings than through his sermons: "And ye became followers of us, and of the Lord, having received the word in much affliction, with joy of the Holy Ghost: so that ye were ensamples to all that believe in Macedonia and Achaia" (1 Thess. 1:6, 7).

Ten-year-old Vaughn Terrell loved the country where he grew up. He finished a big breakfast, then listened to his father read the Scriptures and pray. Afterward he and his older brothers headed for the woods to gather firewood.

While the older boys were working, young Vaughn found a bed of embers left by some hunters the night before. He got down on his knees to blow the embers into flame, not knowing that someone had thrown dynamite caps onto them. Suddenly the caps exploded, knocking Vaughn unconscious.

For days Vaughn was unconscious, near death, during which time his mother never left his side. When he did regain consciousness he was blind, and one of his eyes had to be removed surgically. His whole life-style had to change. He could no longer play with the other children. All he had to sustain him was loving parents and the knowledge that he had received Christ as his Savior two years before. At twelve, he was sent away to the Georgia Academy for the blind. The first semester was hard, as he had never been away from home without his parents.

Graduation from the academy was a thrill but also frightening, because in those days very few blind people were able to support themselves. He couldn't find a job, so during that first summer, he made one for himself—splitting firewood. Being blind, and not needing daylight, he often worked well into the night.

Vaughn had always been interested in studying law, and with a Rotary Club scholarship entered law classes. He immediately ran into difficulty because one of his instructors simply couldn't believe Vaughn would ever be able to succeed in the practice of law. He felt Vaughn would never get past "the technical points." The instructor made life pretty miserable for Vaughn by embarrassing him before the whole class.

Eight months after being admitted to the bar association, Vaughn tried his first case, and it happened that his former instructor was the attorney for the opposition, the very man who had said Vaughn would never practice law successfully. The case had been court-appointed to Vaughn, so there would be no money involved for him. But Vaughn won the case on "a technical point," a case which created a great amount of publicity for him. It was the beginning of a long and highly successful law practice which ended in his being elected district attorney and later to the Georgia legislature.

Vaughn's successes allowed him to introduce the passage of legislation providing for Georgia's Factories for the Blind, giving hundreds of people the opportunity to be self-supporting. More importantly, his life has provided an example that out of suffering can come a life of encouragement to others who have the same kind of suffering to endure.

LESSONS FROM PAUL

Paul challenged his followers to "be ye followers of me, even as I also am of Christ" (1 Cor. 11:1). The Christians at Thessalonica, according to Paul's words, "became followers of us, and of the Lord, having received the word in much affliction, with joy of the Holy Ghost" (1 Thess. 1:6). Those who have taken Paul's words seriously have learned many lessons about suffering.

Rejoice while in your suffering. Paul said, "Rejoice in the Lord alway: and again I say, Rejoice" (Phil. 4:4). These words come from a man who suffered greatly.

I read the Book of Acts regularly and have, on occasion, preached through the book to my congregation. I always receive encouragement as I look again at the early church and its dynamic growth. Its followers grew from 120 the first day to more than three thousand, then more than eight thousand, and soon to an unnumbered multitude all over the

Mediterranean basin. The secret of this amazing growth and accomplishment was their wonderful ability to turn persecution into praise. "And when they had called the apostles, and beaten them, they commanded that they should not speak in the name of Jesus, and let them go. And they departed from the presence of the council, rejoicing that they were counted worthy to suffer shame for his name" (Acts 5:40, 41).

In a day when flashy-dressed Christian musicians are singing and playing and selling their recordings all around the world, I often think of that first sacred concert held in Europe. It was at midnight, in a prison dungeon, as Paul and Silas sang praises to God. I'm not sure what would have happened if many of us had been with Paul that night. Perhaps Paul would have had to sing a solo. We don't know anything about what music they used or what they sang. But I think we can be pretty certain that it wasn't anything like "It's not an easy road," or "Nobody knows the trouble I've seen!" The writer of Acts said, "Paul and Silas prayed, and sang praises unto God: and the prisoners heard them" (Acts 16:25).

Don't act like a martyr. A story is told of a Pennsylvania farmer who was rescued during the terrible Johnstown flood of the nineteenth century. For years after, he would tell the frightful tale to as many as would listen to him. Each time he stressed how much he had suffered through the flood until his rescuers arrived.

According to the story, the man died and went to heaven. With growing impatience, the farmer awaited the hour when he could tell his terrible flood story. The day came for him, and he was very excited—until he noticed that appearing on the list just before him was Noah!

In each recounting of his suffering, Paul was quick to give glory to God and to praise him for finding his suffering useful in the furtherance of the gospel. Paul's testimony was never to incite a pity-party for himself but to give glory to God.

Most believers shy away from needless pain and suffering, but there seem to be some who actually enjoy discomfort, perhaps to generate sympathy and attention to themselves. Others use their sufferings as an occasion for self-pity. Paul spoke of his sufferings, but it was to show the grace of God. His accounts were a far cry from the "organ recitals" we are tempted to offer concerning our accidents, our surgical operations, our hospital stays.

Again, God does not lead where he cannot supply. Since this is true, it is understandable that on occasion God will want to prove himself to us and those around us by putting us in situations where his grace will be needed. As in Job's case, he will do so because he trusts us. At such times, it would be more appropriate for us to take such times of suffering as a compliment, rather than take them as insults, as we sometimes do.

God is in complete control of his universe in all places and at all times. He allows suffering, according to his sovereign will, because he can work out bad situations for something infinitely better, from his viewpoint and ours.

A very popular book was published recently dealing with the topic of suffering. *When Bad Things Happen to Good People,* by Rabbi Harold S. Kushner (New York: Avon, 1981), describes God as limited, and at times, frustrated in his attempts to comfort us in sorrow, as helpless as the ones in need. Kushner wrote: "I believe in God. But I do not believe the same things about Him that I did years ago. . . . I recognize his limitations. He is limited in what he can do by laws of nature and by the evolution of human nature and human moral freedom. I no longer hold God responsible for illnesses, accidents, and natural disasters, because I realize that I gain little and I lose so much when I blame God for those things. I can worship a God who hates suffering but cannot eliminate it. . . ."

While it is true that God generally works within the natural laws he has established, to say that God has no control over human suffering is clearly not the biblical view of God's sovereignty. Paul wrote that "all things work together for good to them that love God, to them who are the called according to his purpose" (Rom. 8:28). It is important to see that Paul did not say all things are good, but that all things *work together for* good.

Certainly, Job would not say that his suffering was good, but we can see that God worked it for good. In the same way, the sufferings we undergo can't in themselves be called good, but in the hands of a sovereign God, all things can be ordered to bring great blessing to ourselves and to others.

CHAPTER SEVEN

When We Suffer

IN chapter one, we looked at a number of reasons why Christians suffer. We suffer because of our fallen nature, because of ungodly people, because of the world system, because of satanic activity, and because of things other Christians do to us.

Perhaps you noticed that we left out one very common reason for our suffering, a reason we don't like to think too much about or even remind our suffering friends about. A very common reason for suffering is simply that we suffer because we deserve to suffer, because of the consequences of our own sin and failure.

SUFFERING FOR THE WRONG REASONS

Sin always has consequences. Sometimes we have to suffer for our failures here on earth. Others will have to suffer in eternity because of their sin and failure. The eternal consequences of the believer's sins were borne, once for all, for us on the cross, when Christ became our sin bearer and our Savior from sin's penalty. Apart from the eternal consequences of sin, it is sometimes true that God delivers us from the earthly consequences of our sins as well. Not all of the bad things that could happen to us actually occur; this is because of divine intervention. In any case, however, someone must bear the consequences of our sins—either us or Christ. Often the result is physical suffering. Someone has said that God had only one sinless Son, but none who didn't suffer.

In the same way that God has linked together holiness and happiness, so has he put together sinfulness and suffering. Paul wrote, "Be not deceived; God is not mocked: for whatsoever a man soweth, that shall he also reap. For he that soweth to his flesh shall of the flesh reap corruption; but he that soweth to the Spirit shall of the Spirit reap life everlasting" (Gal. 6:7, 8).

Peter wrote, "For the time is come that judgment must begin at the house of God: and if it first begin at us, what shall the end be of them that obey not the gospel of God?" (1 Pet. 4:17).

What both Peter and Paul were saying is that there is a spiritual law of retribution, that we reap just what we sow. Sometimes we forget this divine law. Our confession of sin assures us of God's forgiveness (1 John 1:9), but it does not always remove the consequences. A man can push a boulder off a cliff, be immediately sorry for the act, ask forgiveness, and even be forgiven. But it will not necessarily stop the boulder from rolling down the slope and destroying lives and property along the way. Sin has consequences, for us and for those who fall into its path.

If a Christian leader is guilty of immorality, even though he is cleansed by the blood of Christ, he may discover his effectiveness in the community is never the same again. The Bible tells some wonderful stories of forgiveness and restitution, but the warnings of

Scripture are given to remind us that no one can expect to sin with impunity.

Suffering keeps us from sinning. The Apostle Paul wrote: "And lest I should be exalted above measure through the abundance of the revelations, there was given to me a thorn in the flesh . . ." (2 Cor. 12:7). Earlier we talked about Paul's suffering. Theologians have debated for centuries over the nature of the apostle's "thorn," but there is no uncertainty whatsoever about the reason for his infirmity. It was to keep Paul from pride. Before he understood the divine purpose for this suffering, he asked that God would take it away. But when he realized its purpose he concluded: "Most gladly therefore will I rather glory in my infirmities" (2 Cor. 12:9).

Such suffering is not unlike the immunization vaccines given to prevent disease. The needle may sting for a moment, but the pain is nothing compared to the terribly crippling effects of the actual disease the vaccine is designed to prevent.

Suffering makes us confess our sin. The Bible is very clear in its description of David's sin of adultery and murder. It seems that almost a year went by before the sin was confessed to God. The words of Psalms 51 and 32 seem to be the very words David used in his prayers of confession, or at least these were the words he recorded later on.

If we understand the words of Psalm 32 correctly, David must have suffered greatly from feelings of guilt. While others may have been unaware of his sin, David's conscience would never let him forget. He wrote: "When I kept silence, my bones waxed old through my roaring all the day long. For day and night thy hand was heavy upon me: my moisture is turned into the drought of summer" (Ps. 32:3, 4). Though David, when confronted by the prophet Nathan, finally admitted to his sins, for the rest of his life he struggled with an unhappy household, rebellious children—one sadness after another, including one daughter being raped, and two sons killed. Sin has its consequences. Without the suffering that accompanies sin, some would never turn from it.

All through the pages of Scripture we see this principle at work. The entire Book of Judges is the recounting of Israel's sin and God's punishment that came to make them turn away from their sins. "And the children of Israel did evil again in the sight of the Lord. . . . And the anger of the Lord was hot against Israel, and he sold them into the hands of the Philistines, and into the hands of the children of Ammon. . . . And the children of Israel said unto the Lord, We have sinned: do thou unto us whatsoever seemeth good unto thee; deliver us only, we pray thee, this day. And they put away the strange gods from among them, and served the Lord: and his soul was grieved for the misery of Israel" (Judges 10:6, 7, 15, 16). This cycle is repeated some seven times in the Judges—sin, punishment, repentance, restoration, sin. . . .

The prophets give the same messages: "I will go and return to my place, till they acknowledge their offence, and seek my face: in their affliction they will seek me early" (Hosea 5:15). Hosea urged the people to understand the nature of their punishment: "Come, and let us return unto the Lord: for he hath torn, and he will heal us; he hath smitten, and he will bind us up" (Hosea 6:1).

A loving father chastens disobedience. Earlier we discussed the reason for chastening. It is above all, a mark of sonship. When a sinner asks Christ to save him, he is immediately joined to the family of God. He becomes a member of the household of faith. "Now therefore ye are no more strangers and foreigners, but fellowcitizens with the saints, and of the household of God" (Eph. 2:19). But lest we forget, the head of this household, this home, is our heavenly Father, who has laid down certain rules of behavior. If these rules are ignored or broken, divine discipline follows. The writer of Hebrews made this very clear: "My son, despise not thou the chastening of the Lord, nor faint when thou art rebuked of him: For whom the Lord loveth he chasteneth, and scourgeth every son whom he receiveth" (Heb. 12:5, 6). Beware of any teacher or leader who says that because we are Christians we can do anything we like and never worry about being punished. God loves us too much to let us get away with disobedience that disrupts harmony in his home.

When God punishes our disobedience in order to bring us to turn from sins, it doesn't mean that we will then be less fruitful in our work for him. In fact, it can mean the very opposite. When God has burned away the dross, or pruned the unfruitful areas of our lives, it may mean that we are able to produce more fruit. But the one fact remains—one reason for suffering is that God punishes disobedient children. No parent who loves his children will leave them undisciplined.

SUFFERING IN VAIN

There seem to be at least three wrong ways to suffer, according to Peter, who wrote: "For what glory is it, if, when ye be buffeted for your faults, ye shall take it patiently? but if, when ye do well, and suffer for it, ye take it patiently, this is acceptable with God" (1 Pet. 2:20).

Suffering needlessly. It is possible to be in a painful situation, lose sight of God, and start complaining. This kind of suffering doesn't accomplish anything. Peter was trying to encourage those who were suffering, even at the hands of unjust masters. He wrote: "For this is thankworthy, if a man for conscience toward God endure grief, suffering wrongfully" (1 Pet. 2:19).

Calling punishment godly suffering. Another needless form of suffering is the kind we bring on ourselves because of our sins. Again Peter wrote: "But let none of you suffer as a murderer, or as a thief, or as an evildoer, or as a busybody in other men's matters. Yet if any man suffer as a Christian, let him not be ashamed; but let him glorify God on this behalf" (1 Pet. 4:15, 16).

It is easy to confuse the causes of our suffering. We should never hide behind our good motives to cover up our bad behavior shown in carrying out our otherwise good deeds.

One of my pastor friends is talented, zealous, and really loves people. He sometimes tends to be a bit tactless, however, and on occasion his harsh, abrupt manner gets him into trouble. To his credit, my friend is fully aware of these shortcomings, and tries to deal with them. When some unfavorable comment is made about this, he reacts by asking himself whether the criticism is the result of his *position* or his *disposition*, his motives or the way he went about what he was doing, because of something he said, or the way he said it. If he thinks the bad comments are because of his stand on some issue which he believes to be a biblical position, he prays, thanking God for allowing him to suffer for righteousness' sake. But if he thinks the criticism stems from his harshness, he kneels and prays, asking God to forgive him for the needless suffering he has caused himself and others. Then he seeks forgiveness of the one he has offended.

Self-inflicted suffering is useless. Throughout history certain people have been influenced by the so-called "cult of pain," those who believe that some spiritual good is derived from physical suffering. One four-teenth-century mystic, Henry Susa, was said to have worn between his shoulders a cross embedded with iron nails that dug into his flesh. He wore a horsehair shirt with straps in it that held five hundred sharp points which pressed against his skin. Even his gloves were filled with pins. He often beat himself with whips until the blood flowed. All this he did because he believed his suffering bestowed something sacred upon him. Others throughout history emasculated them-selves, thinking it would make discipleship certain.

Suffering, in itself, has no value. We should not seek it nor enjoy it. Self-induced suffering becomes an instrument of Satan to produce spiritual pride. Why else would one inflict suffering upon himself if not in an attempt to pay for some of his own sins, a sacrifice only the sinless Son of God could make for us? There is only one man whose blood was sufficient to pay for our sins, and that is Christ.

How, then, do we suffer needlessly? By doing what God tells us not to do, or by not doing what he tells us to do. We suffer needlessly when we try to bear our

own sins and suffer for them ourselves. The poet
Thomas Baird wrote:

It is His will that I should cast my cares on Him each
   day.
He also bids me not to cast my confidence away.
But oh, how foolishly I act, when taken unawares,
I cast away my confidence, and carry all my cares!

THE GOOD SIDE OF SUFFERING

When Job was suffering he remembered something
about the way God works. He said, "But he knoweth
the way that I take: when he hath tried me, I shall
come forth as gold" (Job 23:10).

Suffering purifies us. Someone said that a plain bar of
ordinary steel brings about ten dollars on the open
market. If the steel is made into horseshoes the price of
the material rises to about twenty-five dollars. But if
this identical ten-dollar bar of steel is made into
delicate springs for expensive watches the market value
could reach a staggering half-million dollars.

This universal principle of multiplication through
purification is seen in various areas. There are some
flowers that will not yield their perfume unless they are
bruised. There is no diamond which is formed without
the heat and pressure of the earth upon it.

William Penn once said: "No pain, no palm; no
thorns, no throne; no gall, no glory; no cross, no
crown." We must remember, when things are rough,
that it is the rubbing and tumbling of stones against
abrasives that bring out their luster and shine. Talents
rise out of adversities, not prosperous circumstances.
Kites rise only when going against the wind.

The Psalmist wrote: "For thou, O God, hast proved us: thou hast tried us, as silver is tried. Thou broughtest us into the net; thou laidst affliction upon our loins. Thou hast caused men to ride over our heads; we went through fire and through water: but thou broughtest us out into a wealthy place" (Ps. 66:10-12). Suffering purifies.

Peter wrote, "That the trial of your faith, being much more precious than of gold that perisheth, though it be tried with fire, might be found unto praise and honour and glory at the appearing of Jesus Christ" (1 Pet. 1:7).

It fulfills the call to suffering. According to Peter, suffering might be considered a special calling. "For even hereunto were ye called: Because Christ also suffered for us, leaving us an example, that ye should follow his steps" (1 Pet. 2:21). In the same vain, Paul wrote, "For unto you it is given in the behalf of Christ, not only to believe on him, but also to suffer for his sake" (Phil. 1:29).

The idea of suffering for Christ's sake is something that could easily be misunderstood. We should never attempt to bring suffering on ourselves, but clearly the Scripture shows that when suffering does come, it might be something God is allowing.

I doubt that any of us will ever be called on to do what God asked Hosea to do. None of us will ever feel the heartache he was asked to endure in order to get across God's message. A brokenhearted lover as Hosea was could tell about a brokenhearted God, whose wife Israel had forsaken him. But remember it was God who asked him to become the object lesson— it wasn't Hosea's idea.

I am always happy when I see young people at missionary conferences dedicate their lives to serve the

Lord. It is a thrill to hear them say, "I now know that God has called me to the ministry," or "During the recent missions conference, I felt God's clear call to serve him in Africa."

Those of us a little older in the faith need to remind these zealous young servants of Christ that there is also the call to suffer. While the Christian life is the most glorious possible life here on earth, it is decidedly not the easiest. A battleground, and not a playground, awaits us when we begin to serve the Lord.

The parable of the sower in Matthew 13 tells of four kinds of soil into which the good seed falls. Each soil is representative of different kinds of people who hear the Word of God. The first group suffers satanic oppression, another suffers tribulation and persecution, and the third group is hindered by worldly care and the deceitfulness of riches. Each of these meet with unexpected persecution or oppression. Some might see from this an important truth about suffering, which might explain the success of the group that heard and understood and brought forth good fruit. Persecution and pain should not surprise us, for we are called to suffer.

Suffering produces fruit. It has been my experience through many years of seeing God at work in the lives of others, that the stronger one's call to suffer, the more productive one's ministry becomes. The two seem directly and inseparably connected. One of the most fascinating books in my library is about the lives of Christian hymnwriters and the stories behind their poetry and music. It is no accident, I believe, that many of our most beloved hymns have poured forth from lives that have undergone immeasurable pain.

H. G. Spafford, who wrote the words to "It Is Well

with My Soul," sent his family ahead of him to Europe.
He was to follow two weeks later. The ship sank and
his four children were drowned. Mrs. Spafford, who
was rescued sent him a cable, "Saved alone." Shortly
before he lost his family, he had lost almost everything
he owned in the Chicago fire. Out of great tragedy and
personal suffering came forth words that have
comforted millions.

P. P. Bliss, who composed the music for "It Is Well
with My Soul," took a train with his wife for Chicago
shortly after he had finished it. They were going there
from Buffalo, New York, to conduct the music for a
series of meetings to be held in Chicago. A bridge gave
way near Ashtabula, Ohio, and more than one hundred
people on the train were killed. P. P. Bliss, someone
reported, could have been saved, but stayed with his
wife, trying to free her from the wreckage, and both of
them were swept up in the flames.

Another of our favorite hymns, "O Love That Wilt
Not Let Me Go," was written by George Matheson, who
was blind. Fanny Crosby, the blind poet, allowed
hundreds of hymn lyrics to flow from her heart,
because she also understood that suffering can be the
source of blessing to others. There is no question that
God has permitted some of these so-called tragedies to
come to people whom he could trust to suffer for the
sake of comforting others.

Dr. Gerald Kroll is director of Pastoral Training at
Liberty Baptist College. He and his wife knew that
hemophilia ran in her family, but they felt God wanted
to give them children, and they believed also that God
could give them a healthy child. For nine months he
and his wife Linda prayed, "Please, God, don't let our
child be a hemophiliac." But Linda gave birth to Bryan,
and six weeks later, at Boston Children's Hospital, his

blood was tested and he was diagnosed as a classic hemophiliac.

Gerald was then a second year seminary student. He became discouraged, feeling God had let him down. To him it seemed that God was allowing an innocent child to suffer, punishing their son for some sin he or his wife had committed. God had answered their prayers in the very opposite way that they had asked.

Doubts flooded Gerald's and Linda's minds during the following months. Gerald had been assigned by his seminary to preach for two weeks in a little church in Maine. Still angry with God, he drove up to fulfill his assignment, not really wanting to do so, but trying to live up to the standards his parents had taught him about fulfilling responsibilities. All the way up to Maine, in his car, Gerald wept and argued with God.

Of that difficult time Gerald wrote: "Then God broke my heart. I simply cried out to God, telling him that I didn't know why he had allowed our son to have hemophilia, but then I didn't know why he had saved me either. 'If you will forgive me of my bitterness, I'll serve you for the rest of my life,' I prayed. It was then that real peace came.

"The sermon that day was different from any I ever preached before, because it had been tried in the fire and had come out purified steel. I have never doubted the Bible or its fundamental truths since that day.

"Passive acceptance of God's will is not enough," Gerald wrote. "Before the suffering that we endure can become a blessing to others, we must commit it to God, accept it as a special calling, and allow God to fill us with grace to endure it. From that sacrifice, God can pour forth comfort to others."

CHAPTER EIGHT

Some Things Are Certain

DURING his years in office, I developed a friendship with Prime Minister Menachem Begin, and shared a number of confidences with him. One day, in talking to this remarkable man, I asked him if there was any secret to the successes of the Israeli armies, who have been more than once victorious on the battlefields. I learned from him and from other Israeli officials that the secret is in the bravery of their soldiers and especially the troop commanders. As a battle is entered, there are two words no Israeli military leader will use: "Forward march!" Instead, the soldiers hear, "Follow me!" In other words, Israeli troops are not *sent* into battle—they are *led* there.

HE IS WITH US

Of some things we can always be certain. One of these truths is that Jesus has not sent us out to suffer alone. Jesus, the One who bore the ultimate in suffering and pain, has not only set the example but goes on before us and with us as we suffer. In every trying moment, he is there. Again, I say, the will of God will never send us where the grace of God cannot sustain us.

A pastor was preaching on the twenty-third Psalm.

He asked if there might be some boy or girl in the audience who could recite the psalm from memory. After some hesitation a very small girl raised her hand and quickly ran to the platform before her surprised parents could stop her.

Considering how young she was, the pastor asked, "Honey, can you really say the twenty-third Psalm?" When she assured him that she could, he lifted her up to the pulpit so everyone could hear.

She began, "The Lord's my shepherd, and that's all I want!" With that she motioned him to put her down, and she ran back to her parents.

Amidst the applause and laughter, the pastor said, "Well, that was a trifle short but I must agree that, from a theological perspective, you have just heard the twenty-third Psalm!"

Perhaps King David would have concurred. The point he was stressing was that, regardless of the dangers confronting him, he would not fear, "for thou art with me; thy rod and thy staff they comfort me" (v. 4). There is a tremendous difference between knowing the psalm about the Good Shepherd and knowing the Good Shepherd himself!

Jesus said, "I am the good shepherd: the good shepherd giveth his life for the sheep" (John 10:11). The shepherd never sends his sheep out alone. "And when he putteth forth his own sheep, he goeth before them, and the sheep follow him: for they know his voice" (John 10:4).

We are never alone in our suffering. Time after time, we see this truth reflected in the Scriptures. Jacob said, "Surely the Lord is in this place; and I knew it not" (Gen. 28:16). This assurance came to someone who had to flee his own home to preserve his life.

We read later in Genesis: "But the Lord was with Joseph, and shewed him mercy" (Gen. 39:21). This expression of God's nearness was given to one who had been sold into slavery by his own brothers.

Moses seemed frightened, overwhelmed by the task God had given him of leading the people of Israel out of Egypt. But God told him, "My presence shall go with thee, and I will give thee rest" (Ex. 33:14).

Men were plotting to take Paul's life. Pressures were coming in on him from all sides. But we read: "Then spake the Lord to Paul in the night by a vision, Be not afraid, but speak, and hold not thy peace: For I am with thee, and no man shall set on thee to hurt thee" (Acts 18:9, 10).

To the whole frightened nation of Israel God said, "The Lord your God which goeth before you, he shall fight for you, according to all that he did for you in Egypt before your eyes" (Deut. 1:30).

GOD KNOWS

God is with us in our suffering. Another truth of which we can be certain is that God knows everything. He knows us, and he knows about the suffering we are undergoing.

Moses reported: "And the Lord said, I have surely seen the affliction of my people which are in Egypt, and have heard their cry by reason of their taskmasters; for I know their sorrows" (Ex. 3:7).

Paul wrote: "Nevertheless the foundation of God standeth sure, having this seal, The Lord knoweth them that are his" (2 Tim. 2:19).

Imagine that an eccentric millionaire hired you to work for him. Suppose he gave you a thimble filled with sand and asked you to count every grain in the thimble. Needing the money, you agree to do the job. Finally, after many weary, eye-straining hours, you finish the job and report the total to him, a sum so large you can hardly keep track of the zeros.

Then imagine he gives the thimble of sand back to you and says, "Now, give each one of these grains of sand a name." I wonder if you or anyone else would accept such a ridiculous job. But scientists tell us that there are as many stars in the universe as there are grains of sand on the many seashores of the world. The Psalmist recorded, "He telleth the number of the stars; he calleth them all by their names" (Ps. 147:4).

But that is not the best part. The same God who numbers and names the untold trillions of stars has expressed his desire to comfort us in all our sorrows. In fact, this great truth appears in the very same psalm: "He healeth the broken in heart, and bindeth up their wounds" (Ps. 147:3).

HE NOTICES OUR TEARS

One of the tenderest truths we can learn about God is found in one of David's psalms. David wrote, "Thou tellest my wanderings: put thou my tears into thy bottle: are they not in thy book?" (Ps. 56:8). These are words that should comfort and cheer the most despondent heart. In this verse, David expressed his belief that God's nearness to him and his care for him are so intimate that God would count and preserve all his tears.

This psalm seems to say that God not only sees our tears but seems willing to allow us to weep when we are hurting. Many Christians, I believe, have wrongly advised those who are suffering that it is wrong to show grief, no matter how much they are hurting, because it is a sign of unbelief.

Dave Adams is one of the pastors at Thomas Road Baptist Church. His son Joshua was born with heart problems. It wasn't easy for the young parents, Dave and Becky, to watch their six-month-old son and see the terror in his eyes as he was strapped down to X-ray tables. The little boy was in and out of the hospital many times during the following months.

When Joshua was four and a half years old they took him back to the hospital in Charlottesville, this time for open heart surgery. Carrying his son from his second-floor room to surgery, Dave knew it could be the last time he would see him alive. The ten-minute walk seemed like a painful eternity. Josh was given some medication to prepare him for surgery, and just before the anesthesiologist came into the waiting room to take him to surgery, Josh nodded off to sleep in his father's arms.

The doctor disappeared through the doors, carrying Josh in his arms. Dave and Becky embraced, the pain in their hearts seemed unbearable. There was nothing left to do or say.

They went to the special waiting room provided for immediate relatives, where others were also waiting for loved ones who were undergoing surgery. Dave later wrote of that moment: "I became aware of the intense bond that I had with several other people waiting there, the fellowship of suffering for a loved one going through difficulty."

After a long wait, they learned that the surgery had been successful. Even though the hospital staff had tried to explain to them what Josh would look like after surgery, neither Dave nor Becky was prepared to see their tiny son connected to all kinds of tubes, wires, and breathing devices running in and out of him. It was impossible for a loving parent to see such a sight without feeling deep pain themselves.

"Oh, God," Dave cried. "I wish it were me." He said later that he never knew it was possible for him to feel such empathy as this, feelings that stretched him to near exhaustion.

Dave said later, "During Josh's surgery and painful recovery, I learned that it is acceptable to communicate pain and it is important to lean on those who are stronger."

Our tears *are* seen by God! He *does* feel our pain. The Son of God, who wept beside the tomb of Lazarus, a friend whom he loved, and who wept outside of Jerusalem for people he loved, can certainly understand and appreciate our tears. He knows when our grief reflects unbelief and distrust. But he also knows when our grief is genuine and when it reflects our dependence on him. The One who puts tears in a bottle can know the difference.

SUFFERING WILL SOMEDAY BE OVER

Some things continue for ever. Peter wrote, "The word of the Lord endureth for ever" (1 Pet. 1:25). The name of God abides forever (Ps. 72:17). God's glory is eternal (Ps. 104:31). Other things can be added to this "everlasting" list, but the suffering of the saints is not one of them!

Throughout the Scriptures we are given such promises as "For his anger endureth but a moment; in his favour is life: weeping may endure for a night, but joy cometh in the morning" (Ps. 30:5).

Isaiah wrote, "The days of thy mourning shall be ended" (Isa. 60:20).

Paul wrote, "For our light affliction, which is but for a moment, worketh for us a far more exceeding and eternal weight of glory; while we look not at the things which are seen, but at the things which are not seen: for the things which are seen are temporal; but the things which are not seen are eternal" (2 Cor. 4:17, 18).

I once heard a minister say, "I must be honest in saying I no longer believe in a future sky-high heaven or in a red-hot hell. I believe instead that both heaven and hell are experienced here on earth alone." As strange as it may sound, I agree with this liberal minister, from one small perspective. Without being the least bit aware of it, he had stated a profound truth.

For the person who is not a believer and never becomes a believer, this world, with the good things that are to be experienced here, is the only "heaven" he will ever know. To that person who will never experience the joys of eternal heaven, we might say, "Live it up, friend. Do your own thing. Eat, drink, and be merry, but remember, this is all the 'heaven' you will ever know."

For the person who receives Christ and enters into the fellowship of his suffering here on earth, it is the only pain and suffering—the only "hell"—he will ever know. Here on earth, Satan is allowed, with God's permission, to inflict some suffering on us. But someday all of that will be over, eternally. And God will wipe all tears from our eyes!

There is a story of two boys who grew up in the same neighborhood, attended the same school, and went to the same college. One young man received

Christ during his sophomore year. Upon graduation the
two men went their separate ways. One went to law
school. The Christian went to the mission field.

Twenty years passed and both men were arriving
home. The missionary's wife and his two children had
died and were buried on the mission field, stricken
down with tropical diseases. The missionary decided to
visit his old home town. As his train pulled into the
station, he noticed a crowd of people with large banners
which read, "Welcome Home."

It didn't take him long to realize that the signs were
not for him but for his former classmate, who had
recently been elected governor of the state. He was
arriving "home" on the same train.

During the celebration, the missionary slipped out of
the noisy crowd and went to his cheap, darkened hotel
room, which overlooked the festivities below.

He might have said, "Some things down here are
hard to understand. I have sacrificed my family, my
health, my very life for the cause of Christ. But here I
sit in this lonely room, not knowing what my next step
should be. But my old friend, who has little regard for
spiritual things—look what is happening to him."

But that is not the end of the story. The governor was
arriving home to receive all the acclaim he was ever
going to receive. For the missionary, the story was not
over. He had not yet arrived "home."

I once did a study of all the Scriptures, tracing the
trail of tears across the pages of the Bible. What a study
it was! The trail leads from Genesis through all the Old
and New Testament books, reaching its crest in the
Book of Revelation.

The tears begin in the Garden with the Fall. They
continue at the death of Abel. The trickle continues,

being fed by the tears of Jacob for Joseph, of Moses for Miriam, of Hannah for her son, of Samuel for Saul. It continues in David's weeping over his sins, weeping for his children, for his son Absalom. The prophets wept over Israel and Judah, and Paul wept over his unbelieving countrymen.

The trail of tears continues as Mary wept at the tomb. The stream finds itself carrying the most precious tears of all, as Jesus weeps over Lazarus and finally over Jerusalem.

But at last, in the Book of Revelation, the swollen sea is dramatically and decisively stopped. The last recorded tears of the believer are found in Revelation 5:5, when the elders say: "Weep not: behold, the Lion of the tribe of Juda, the Root of David, hath prevailed." We see the last of them in chapter 21: "And God shall wipe away all tears from their eyes; and there shall be no more death, neither sorrow, nor crying, neither shall there be any more pain: for the former things are passed away" (Rev. 21:4).